About the Author

Remy Bernier started a new life in 2006. This was the result of a terrible event that would change his life forever: Remy had suffered a stroke. Prior to his accident, he was thriving as an aspiring mountain guide. Now, the right hemisphere of Remy's body is paralyzed, and his coordination, speech and vision have been affected. He will be in a wheelchair for the rest of his life. This memoir took him seven years to write, because he could only type with one finger. He continues to raise the bar in everything he does and has no plans to stop!

Author note: I'm far from being a writer, and I never pretend to be one. My book is not perfect. If you have difficulty following, so be it! Editors from Olympia had a big challenge with my manuscript. I'm the black sheep who did not want to make the corrections. I have a unique style, and I don't want to lose that.

From Mountaineer to Stroke Survivor — Never Give Up

Remy Bernier

From Mountaineer to Stroke Survivor —
Never Give Up

Olympia Publishers
London

www.olympiapublishers.com
OLYMPIA PAPERBACK EDITION

Copyright © Remy Bernier 2021

The right of Remy Bernier to be identified as author of
this work has been asserted in accordance with sections 77 and 78
of the Copyright, Designs and Patents Act 1988.

All Rights Reserved

No reproduction, copy or transmission of this publication
may be made without written permission.
No paragraph of this publication may be reproduced,
copied or transmitted save with the written permission of the
publisher, or in accordance with the provisions
of the Copyright Act 1956 (as amended).

Any person who commits any unauthorised act in relation to
this publication may be liable to criminal
prosecution and civil claims for damage.

A CIP catalogue record for this title is
available from the British Library.

ISBN: 978-1-78830-813-7

First Published in 2021

Olympia Publishers
Tallis House
2 Tallis Street
London
EC4Y 0AB
Printed in Great Britain

Dedication

For Doctor Nuts:
He was so smart that he didn't see the difference between a perfectly healthy person and a manic.

Acknowledgements

To me:
Because I believed in the project, and if I had listened to anyone else, this book would have been dead long ago.

October 18th, 2006

Where am I? Why am I in a bed? I'm not at home… why can I see from only one eye? And why do I see so poorly from that eye? What is the tubing sticking out from my belly? Why can't I move my right arm? I just need to stand up, but wait a minute, I can't. This must be a hospital bed. Here we go. I recognize the woman walking up to me, it's Jacynthe, my wife. I'm going to ask her what is going on.

Great… I can't even speak. She is telling me that I had a stroke. Apparently, I have been awake for two weeks, but I can only remember this morning. The speech therapist is passing by.

I need to make some noise. This is tough! Now, she is gone.

Rewind

What can I remember? I know! I was on the phone discussing my project to climb Mount Everest. I was excited, and my blood pressure was though the roof. After I hung up I began to feel a numbness throughout my right side. I called my wife and she told me that I was having a stroke.

That's it! I get it! I had a stroke! So many puzzle pieces to put together. I don't know where to start. At least, I have my wife beside me…

Goodbye?

You're going?

I haven't said anything yet. Wait a minute… I can't say anything! I want to say at very least, goodbye.

Too late, she's gone.

Continued by Chic Scott: Jacynthe (Jass) Brodeur, Remy's ex-wife:

At about four p.m. on October 18, 2006 Remy suffered a hemorrhagic stroke. He was at home at the time and he phoned me and said, "Half my body is numb, and my head is spinning."

He then walked out into the street. Seeing our neighbor, Charlotte, he asked her to take him to the hospital. In the car he said, "I'm fucked. I'm going to die."

Charlotte called 911 and kept driving, meeting the ambulance near the Elk Run RCMP station. They intubated Remy and almost immediately he was flown by helicopter to the Foothills Hospital in Calgary.

Within an hour of his stroke he was in the coma.

We found out that Remy had lived all his life with a silent time bomb in his brain — an arterial venous malformation (AVM). About five centimeters in size, this congenital knot of blood vessels located at the base of his brain had burst and begun to bleed.

Since it was located around the brainstem and so near the breathing and cardiac centers of the brain, there was little the surgeons could do, it was just too risky. They decided to let it bleed until it stopped naturally. This led to severe damage to his brainstem and his cerebellum.

Remy was in a deep coma for almost a month; the first two weeks in the Intensive Care Unit.

At five days Remy began to show signs that he was still conscious: in response to a question, he would squeeze your hand. Slowly, Remy woke up.

On week three he was transferred to the Neural Unit on

the eleventh floor of the hospital. He could now open his eyes and say yes or no by flicking his eyelids. After six weeks, he was transferred to Unit 58, where he went through intensive rehabilitation.

Gradually he began to rebuild his life.

Remy:

I was twenty-seven years old when I had my stroke. I was in a coma for a month and spent another two years in hospitals.

I have no sensation at all in the right hemisphere of my body. This makes it impossible to stand — even for a second — therefore, I am permanently bound to a wheelchair.

My speech and pitch have become so strained that most people don't understand what I am saying.

My vision has also been affected. I see double, so I must block my right eye to help correct my sight. I need giant print (32pts) to read and I can only see detail within ten meters; for example, a friend's face, although I can see the landscape quite far.

I am French Canadian and currently live in Alberta. I began to learn English twenty years ago, and half of those years have been in my current condition. Despite English being my second language, I decided to write my book in English because I want the people I care about, to be able to read my story.

Chapter 1
Growing Up (1979–1989)
A Small Boy

I was born in Montreal, Quebec and grew up in a small town, on the south shore of Saint Lawrence River near Montreal, called Verchères, until I turned seventeen years old. Then, I moved to St-Ferréol-Les-Neiges near Quebec City.

I have one brother eight years older than me. The age gap makes me think that I was likely an unplanned surprise, but my parents always loved me.

There are some days I wonder how my brother tolerated me. In his teenage years, I thought every friend he brought home would automatically be my friend.

For a while, I think he used me as more of a punching bag than anything else. Then one day I discovered that a kick in the private parts was the quickest way to end the fight; I made sure to keep that one on my list of secret weapons.

As we grew older, my brother became my best friend. I owe my love for the outdoors to him as it was he who first introduced me to my outdoor adventures.

When I was a little boy, I loved spending my summers with my grandparents at our family cottage on Grenier Lake in Lanaudière. I was always doing one of three things — fishing, swimming or playing the boy scout in the forest. I was never bored! I was kind of a chubby kid, who liked his cookies a bit too much, but that didn't stop me from swimming for hours straight until my skin looked like a raisin, partly due to my love of water and partly to hide my bit of a tummy.

I joined Louveteaux, the French version of Cubs, at age eight. For three years I was a focused and dedicated member. After my first year, I became the leader of five Cubs. Most Cub members must wait until they complete their second year to receive that honor. By the end of my second year, I had reached the highest ranking possible. There were no badges left for me to earn during my third year.

Even at a young age, I had the drive to put all my energy into a challenge and a focus that refused to quit; a challenge might discourage some but not me.

In the winter of 1987, I was about eight years old and skiing with my dad in Longueuil, Quebec while waiting for my brother to finish his ski club training. I was not yet competitively minded.

At the end of the trail, the club was training by doing intervals, racing as fast as they could in short bursts. Many short races took place in one training session. The coach noticed me and asked if I'd like to join the girls for an interval.

I was excited by the chance to prove myself, and as a child with my brother's second-hand gear (not very high tech compared to the $500 skis that most of the girls had) I joined their race. I did not finish first of course — some of the girls were on the national team — but I did not finish last either. A fourteen-year-old girl even burst into tears, an upsetting sight, but the performance was my ticket and I officially became a member of the racing club the following year.

I grew into a focused teenager. Life was all about cross-country skiing.

It was the Eastern Canadian Championship, near Toronto. Classic style (traditional, skis parallel in two tracks) Saturday and skating style (modern, "v" shape and no track needed) Sunday.

After a bitter performance one Saturday, the kind that leaves a permanent scar in an athlete's career, I surprised myself on the final race of the weekend and bounced back!

Chapter 2
Cross-country Skiing (1988–1998)
Athlete First

In 1994 I competed at the Eastern Canadian Championships North of Toronto. I was feeling the pressure. I needed to do better than yesterday.

It wouldn't be hard because I finished dead last the day before! I felt pressure not only to perform and succeed but I did not want to look like a fool.

This day's race was the ten-kilometer skating style. Yesterday it was the classic style. I tried to put everything about that race out of my mind to avoid getting consumed by the disappointment. It was the only race I finished last in over my ten-year career.

I warmed up and prepared to go to the starting line: three… two… one… Go!

I was surprised. It felt easy… I glided.

I felt excited when I compared how smoothly I was skiing to what I couldn't do the day before. I passed many competitors. It felt like a good sign. And then there was the finish line! I felt hopeful.

At the end of the race, I did my cool-down and tried not to worry about the results as I prepared for the wait.

"Remy! Remy! You won! The results are already out!" In fact, I won with more than a minute between me and second place. If I had competed in the higher category, I would have finished in the top five. I had become a skating style boy.

In the beginning I was a Classic Style skier, as I didn't perform as well in Skating Style. I found I was always on the podium in Classic and never in Skating. During my time as a 'Juvenile' (ages thirteen to fourteen) Skating Style just seemed to be my niche.

I continued to do well as I aged, and even surprised myself by winning a bronze medal at the Canadian Championship in Hull, Quebec in Skating Style.

As I progressed to Junior B, my Classic weakened and my Skating strengthened.

By the time I was competing in Junior A, I had cut out Classic altogether. Although I was a great cross-country skier, I began to realize my focus had changed during the last two years of competing; I had switched from everything cross-country and had expanded into adventure sports.

During my teen years, I traveled all over the country via planes or on long highway drives.

I was training at Mount Ste-Anne near Quebec City, but I was living close to Montreal. My parents bought a cottage to make the commute easier on us. Every weekend, all year, we drove a six-hour round trip to train or compete. My parents were extremely dedicated, and I am so lucky and grateful for the sacrifice and efforts they made for my goals.

In the fall of 1997, just when I moved to Mont-Sainte-Anne to be nearer to my coach, I dropped him for the local team.

I was attending college and I had signed up for an Introduction to Rock Climbing class. I was excited, but a conflict arose between skiing when I found out a training camp was scheduled for the same time.

I had made myself available over years and often at the expense of other activities, and I wasn't prepared to sacrifice this new-found interest. My coach had different ideas: he told me to forget about the rock climbing and that I had more important things to do. I was not willing to budge this time.

Angrily, I explained the situation to my parents. We all decided that it was time to move on. I left the prestigious club Ski-Elite for Mont-Sainte-Anne, a decision I have never regretted.

I progressed from hiking to climbing. My brother showed me a great hiking area. I became an enthusiastic guide for all my friends, dragging them out to places I had newly discovered.

Chapter 3
Adirondacks (1993–1997)
An Adventurer is Born

My brother introduced me to hiking in the Adirondacks when I was fourteen. The place that spawned my budding new passion was found on the American side of the border, just over an hour and a half from where I grew up. Located in New York State, this large network of mountainous trails is a destination for many outdoor enthusiasts but is more often intimately enjoyed by the residents of the Olympic town, Lake Placid.

When I got my license at sixteen, I began to play 'guide' well before I conceived the notion of becoming a professional guide. As an eager young man, I gathered my gear and obsessed about getting out to the mountains, earning the tag "Mr Hiking." In my mind, I knew everything about hiking and I was ready to share the experiences with my friends. I must admit, we had many good trips and some sketchy situations, but that comes with the territory.

At seventeen and eighteen I started to visit the area early in the spring and late in the fall. Not many people were as hard core as I was, but one of my good friends, Jean-Francois Monette, followed me without too much complaint. There were many early mornings in the dark, frigid temperatures, lots of snow melting and frozen boots. To me it was extreme, and I loved it so much. I don't know about my friends, though.

It was early spring 1997 and snow still blanketed the peaks. We drove late through the night and crashed out in the parking lot of the trailhead. Sebastien Ouellette and Jean-Francois Monette and I were eager for an adventure. We were just turning seventeen and were still in high school. We borrowed my mom's car and planned a three-day trip.

We awoke early unhindered from our late night and impromptu camping spot. We hiked all day Saturday and pitched camp on the tree line of Mount Gothic. The fact that the temperature was way below zero didn't freeze our youthful aspirations, but our hiking boots froze solid. We did not melt enough snow to drink, leaving us thirsty. A rough start to a day, but an experience I have since fondly replayed in my mind countless times.

We jammed our feet into our boots and we packed the tent as quickly as we could with frozen fingers. It was going to be another good day, no clouds to be seen.

Less than one minute into day two Sebastien slipped. Sebastien sprained his ankle so badly that he couldn't walk on it.

We went from adventurers to three inexperienced teens stuck on a remote peak in minutes: first aid in the wilderness 101. Since I was the most experienced, I took charge of the situation.

Near the summit, there was some down-scrambling to navigate before we could get to help. We needed a rope. The only rope we had was a small accessory rope good for hanging food to deter bears. Too weak — we would need a rope that could hold body weight, basically a climbing rope.

I asked Jean-Francois to stay with Sebastien while I went down the mountain to get some help, but Sebastien couldn't wait in his frozen boots, he would never warm up without moving around. We didn't need a case of frostbite to add to this misadventure!

We helped Sebastien take off his boots and tucked him into his sleeping bag. Now it was just a matter of how we were going to get him off this mountain?

I ventured off to find help. It felt like a cross-country race, but I was alone. I worried about what I would say if I was lucky enough to find someone. My English was pretty basic and I didn't know if I would be able communicate clearly.

I covered ground quickly, descending alone without a heavy pack, spurred on by my anticipation of finding someone to help. After an hour I ran into two Americans at the Wolf Jaw lean-to. I tried to explain my situation but by the look of it they did not understand.

Unsure of what was lost in translation I continued my trek, determined to get help before we were stuck on the mountain for another night.

There was no one at Adirondack Lodge. It is all closed up for winter and too early in the season to open. I was disappointed as I was really hoping finding someone there. I decided to go back up the mountain and wait with the guys. My parents knew where we were headed and the trails we were planning to take. They would begin to worry when we did not return and would call Search and Rescue.

We would have to simply wait it out.

I climbed back up the trail, defeated and feeling useless. When I reached our makeshift rest spot, I saw that the guys were not alone. It was the two Americans from the lean-to! They were making a call on a cellphone. Help was on the way! The rescue would be fifteen minutes by helicopter.

It would seem that after I continued down the mountain, the Americans decided to hike up to check out the situation. They understood something bad had happened. I had managed to explain the location well enough, but they were confused as to what was wrong exactly. Thank goodness for their concern.

The helicopter arrived, and the rescue team put Sebastien on a long line (attached at the end of a rope underneath the helicopter) and he gets the view of a lifetime as he is flown down the mountain. With Sebastien in good hands, Jean-Francois and I ventured back down to the car.

Back home, I planned my first outdoor, real climbing adventure.

Chapter 4
The Adventure Begins (1997–2000)
Aim to Do It Like the Pros

I was attempting my first traditional climb which was also my first multi-pitch, three pitches to be exact.

Not only that but it was my first lead attempt and my partner had never climbed outside and was inexperienced. Everything I did back then, I am totally against now! Like an old school adventurer, I learned many lessons by trial and error and luckily without too severe an error.

I was full of teen invincibility, too young to anticipate failure. I am experienced enough now to know what could happen out there, and as a responsible climber I leave here my disclaimer: If you are young and strong and believe nothing can happen to you, know that it can. If you want to live a long life full of adventure, please do not make the same mistakes that I did. Find yourself an experienced guide and learn from their training and experience. I am embarrassed by the ignorant risks I took in my youth and I am a bad example of responsible risk taking.

I am just lucky enough to be able to write this book.

I planned to tackle Adagio at Weir without a professional guide and without guidance from someone who had climbed it. I was sure I knew all I needed to know having had memorized my new bible *Mountaineering: Freedom of the*

Hills. It was the new source of my mountaineering day dreams, and I knew by heart every page covering lead climbing and trad climbing.

I now firmly believe that is the only reason I did not die that day. I was arrogant and inexperienced and anybody with experience thought I was reckless. I was boycotted by the climbing community. Fine! I would show them! I would take fresh blood on my journeys.

My partner and I were preparing at the bottom of the climb. I knew my stuff on paper, and now it was time to put my theory to the test. I had studied more for that route than any exam in my entire life. I was not intimidated and would not second guess myself.

With the ignorance and determination of youth, I was hell-bent on making this climb!

The climb was hard for only a 5.8 (5a) grade. And from what I understood, the difficulty of the climb was determined by a grade of "Easy" at 5.4 (4a) to "Very Hard" at 5.15 (9a+).

It was only *after* the climb that I learned about old school grading. This was before 1960, which determined that 5.10 (5c) was determined to be the hardest climb found. It was obvious that the old school climbing grade was way harder than the contemporary grade!

That said, Adagio was definitely old school, having been climbed for the first time in 1959.

I was still very green and had climbed on maybe twelve occasions, and *never* on lead (no safety of the top rope above). And since I hadn't yet mastered the gymnastics of climbing, I had to muscle my way up the cruxes, also known as the difficult parts of a climb. There were times I almost fell but in my stubborn mindset, there was only one way to go, and that was up.

At this point, turning around was not an option, but it didn't matter because I was climbing up no matter what. I could only think to myself that if I fall, hopefully, my protections will hold me.

The exposure and height of the climb were other factors that I did not consider and being on a rock face at eighty meters high can make it very hard to stay focused. And while looking down was terrifying, reaching my goal overcame my fear.

Guess what? The climb went fine! I would have to remember to do the important things like stacking the rope at the belay stations, but I knew those things would come with practice. My focus was now on rock climbing.

When climbing routes, you must have a partner. I only had so many 'beginner' partners who were willing and able and I was still being denied by the experienced climbers. As is often the case with young men who are determined and motivated, I found it hard to find people who were willing to drive long hours after school or on weekends to undergo long slogs for a bit of climbing.

Then I met a guy who told me about aid soloing. This is a type of climbing where the ropes and protections are used to progress on a wall comparable to climbing rock; you only use the protections in a case of a fall. Convincing, he sold me a piece of equipment that I would need to modify for this specific purpose.

As you can probably tell, the guy was slick. He also happened to be a salesman at the biggest outdoor store in Quebec City.

So, I got myself a grigri (the piece of equipment), a

belay device with a cam that holds the rope. Did the modifications on it and I was back on the rock, this time alone, as I was soloing with my new toy. My mom never knew what I was doing but she would have been so upset that I got an expensive piece of gear and just few minutes later was already breaking it with the grinder.

That same summer, I met a special girl. Her name was Jacynthe Brodeur. She was beautiful and athletic. Because I was younger and greener, she felt that I was not up to the task to hang out with her, and she dumped me. (Don't worry, I get her back and she eventually becomes my wife!)

In the meantime, I was determined to bury my love story and become a brand new me. *K2 — The Ultimate Summit* was my favorite movie and I envisioned myself to be like the lawyer. Not very popular with the girls at the start of college, I had a few catches by the time I was completely fed up with school — shy of one course to graduate.

Having my heart broken by Jacynthe, I engraved on a small rock:

"*Jamais, je laisserai l'amour d'une fille compromettre mes reves.*"

Which means in English:

"Never will I let the love of a woman compromise my dreams."

I was a young man really driven by something: cross-country skiing at first, and climbing later on.

Having my heart broken like this, I strongly believed that nobody would be able to stop me. More and more, I was living like the character in K2. That vision would stand until Yukon 2000, when I was back with my first true love. After that I was not the same man — I was turning into a softy!

My newer discovery was individual sports where I was able to challenge myself and give myself an adrenaline rush: sea kayaking, rock climbing, aid climbing, hiking, mountain biking, caving and canyoneering. Later in the winter, I was attracted by expedition style cross-country skiing, ice climbing, Telemark skiing, winter camping and sleeping in igloos.

I became interested in anything that had to do with the outdoors and my favorite place to go was the Outdoor Show at Place Bonaventure, in Montreal. This was a place full of exciting ideas and kept my dreams alive for potential adventure.

At this point, I felt ready for the major leagues! I wanted to tackle some really big mountains! I kept thinking, "Let's go to a really, really big one — the Aconcagua!"

But first, I had to make a change. I started to hang out with the right people. The people who would help me reach this new goal.

Chapter 5
Aconcagua (1997–1998)
Small Boots, Big Mountain!

Aconcagua, Argentina, the summit push! It was so windy, probably more than 100 km/h. I was so close and yet so far. It read 6, 700 meters on my altimeter. The summit at 6, 962 m.

The wind kept pushing me against the slope, holding me hostage. I guess we hadn't picked a good day for our lightweight bodies. Everyone had turned around except the biggest man on our team. Finally, the group had decided that it was time to turn around. They felt that there was no point in even trying to fight against the wind.

Anyway, in a few days, I would get another chance to scale the Polish Glacier.

The plan for Aconcagua was to do our acclimatization on the normal route. We would then climb up the Polish Glacier. We had already dragged the ropes, crampons and ice axes all the way to the base camp. I was sure that we would get another crack at it.

The leader of our team was a big guy, and with his bulk and luck, he had made it to the summit. He did what he had come here to do. He had the most experience and he used the fact that everyone had a hard time to get acclimatized. The troop, hungry and tired, was easily convinced to head down the mountain the next morning.

Everyone except me.

I was not done with the mountain yet. I tried them to stay, explaining that we have only done expedition, by my efforts were useless. After spe...o weeks on the mountain, everyone was tired and just wanted to return to civilization.

Driven by my insatiable need to ascend and my pure inability to quit, I made the ignorant decision to continue by myself. This was a suicidal decision. Any number of things could happen, from avalanches to crevasses, altitude sickness to a small injury. One small mishap and I would have no one to help me.

But the following day, everybody was gone, and I spent the rest of the day resting and lonely. I sure felt small and I sensed guilt at wanting to stick with the original plan. It was too late to reconsider, so I set my alarm clock for three a.m.

I was an eighteen-year-old Quebecer, on a giant mountain in Argentina. I couldn't speak Spanish and my team had retreated to the city of Mendoza. I was alone in a dangerous wonderland. But I was strong and blinded by my drive. I kept saying to myself, "Nothing can happen to me."

I decided to climb a small peak adjacent to the Aconcagua, accessible from the base camp. Mt Cuerno, standing at 5,462 meters, was a ramp filled with crevasses that led to the summit. Since almost everyone at base camp would be heading up the Aconcagua, I knew that there would be no one else around as I attempted to climb this obscure route.

There are unusual snow formations common in the Andes called *penitentes*. These are fascinating spikes that stretch out from the snow. As I made the climb, I found that some were as big as six feet tall and stood in groups of hundreds. They were like hands reaching up from the ground, as if trying to hold me back. The result made for an extravagant maze that I would have to negotiate en route to the summit. I thought to myself, "I will never get over this barrier of snow and ice!" But by perseverance, I managed to get through this obstacle.

Established on the ice fields, I was impressed by some giant holes in the ice. I had climbed all around the world and these were by far the biggest I had come across. Those I had encountered in Alaska were 'small' in comparison.

I had no idea how I would make it through and around this newest obstacle, but I was undaunted and amazingly I made it through. Beginners luck, I guess!

I remember living that a special moment on the summit. I had the best view, for sure, of the Aconcagua. And I could see also from where I started this adventure. The tents were so small and far!

Then I remembered that I was only halfway through completing my journey. I started to trace my way back down the mountain. The penitentes were more savage than on my way up. I was exhausted and if I spoke Spanish, I would order a shopper... Right, I don't have a radio! I wanted to kick myself for being so stupid.

Despite this oversight, I managed to be back at camp sixteen hours later, and without incident. If it weren't for the penitentes, the climb probably would have only taken me about half the time to complete.

Once I made the descent, I went directly to my sleeping bag. I was exhausted!

I don't know how I survived those early years without

any accidents. I had no radio, I hadn't told anyone where I was going. I was on the other side of the planet from my home! It took over a day's worth of trekking to get to the bottom of this mountain and I was now at more than 4, 400 m!

The day after my epic climb, I returned to my friends in Mendoza. Everyone was eagerly awaiting the afternoon bus to find out what had become of me. I stepped off the bus and everybody felt lighter. I sometimes wonder what would they have done if I was not on the bus? Would they have come together and headed up the mountain to try to find me? Would they have amassed a search party? Or would they have fearfully abandoned me and silently felt grateful that they were safe off the mountain?

I am relieved to say that I will never know.

This climbing success would bolster my confidence. It would also lead me to push my luck on the next three expeditions I was about to take.

Chapter 6
Ecuador (1998–1999)
On to the Next One!

After having climbed Cayambe, Illiniza Sur and Cotopaxi in Ecuador, I had failed my attempt on the tallest peak, Chimborazo.

Having become very sick, I was knocked down with bouts of diarrhea and vomiting. As my friends continued toward the summit, I headed back down to the city of Baños feeling defeated. I remember saying to myself, "I'm not done with this mountain. I can't go back home without reaching the highest peak on Earth!"

Even though Everest has the biggest elevation from sea level to its summit, Chimborazo is actually considered the highest point above the center of the Earth. This is because the world is an oval shape and Chimborazo is located near the equator where the Earth's diameter is greatest.

I still had three weeks to go, still plenty of time to get better. I'm more fortunate than the Japanese couple I met. I will tell you their story; it's worth it to spend some extra time on these two wild climbers!

On my way down Chimborazo, I passed a "wild" Japanese couple whom I had met earlier at the hut.

The woman was on her knees and leaving a trail of vomit every 100 meters. Her husband was roped up to his wife and was pulling on the rope as if she were his defiant dog on leash. He was yelling at her in Japanese. I had no idea what he was saying but I could tell it did not sound nice. They returned, six hours later than my friends, having summited.

We all left together at midnight, having climbed during the night to avoid the strong Ecuadorian sun. During the day the snow becomes heavy and the risk of avalanches and *serac* fall was dangerous and scary.

The Japanese couple arrived at the hut just in time to catch a taxi to the Quito airport and jump onto a plane and head home that very night.

Before they left, the husband explained to us that if they returned to their country without bagging the summit they would be shamed. The two of them had only four days off from work and had traveled one and a half days to get to Ecuador. They then took a 260-kilometer taxi ride to the hut, going from sea level to 5, 000 meters in a matter of hours. That left the couple just one night and one morning to climb the mountain.

That was why the woman was so exhausted, and her body was fighting the climb every step of the way.

They then needed to travel all the way back to Japan with just enough time to get back to work the very next day! I don't know anyone else that would commit to crossing half of the globe to climb a mountain on a long weekend. Even after all these years, I am still amazed by their story.

Anyway, it took me a week in Baños to recover from the bug I had caught prior Chimborazo. I spent the time exploring the quaint city and met a young woman from Quebec that had grown up in the next town over from me. We joined forces to trek a small, 5, 023-meter volcano called Tungurahua.

I had heard that this active volcano had erupted a couple

of times since 1999 and climbing and trekking was prohibited during the activity peak due to safety concerns. We decided to check with the Geophysics Institute, since I'm sure we wouldn't want to be near this place during eruption time.

We confirmed that it was safe to make the journey, and it was such a pleasant trek. It started in the jungle, with a high alpine setting at the end. We saw monkeys and lots of pretty flowers at low altitude, traded off by smaller trees as we went up, followed eventually by snow. It was a straightforward mountain for acclimatizing before the big one, Chimborazo.

The next day I took the taxi for the Chimborazo's hut. The mountain had changed since my last trip, having amassed thirty centimeters of fresh snow. I was on my own, but again, I was too blinded by the adventure to consider the fact that I might end up in a crevasse, stranded.

Here we go again — Another classic Remy experience!

As I wrote this book, I came to realize how dumb I was. I would be lying if I said that this was the last time. But don't worry, my bag is still full! There are more stupid decisions to come.

It was two in the morning and, as the first trekker, that would mean having to break the trail on my own.

I felt strong again and thanks to my cross-country legs I was able to break the trail with no issue. I reached the summit and back down in a flash, and then I took the taxi back to Baños where my friends were. After a warm reunion with all the stories of the past week and half, we spent the remainder of our time sightseeing and traveling around Ecuador.

Having made one successful trip out of two, it was time to see if the White Beast (Denali) would take it easy on me.

Chapter 7
Mount McKinley (Denali) (1999)
Strike #...

I was twenty and had decided to climb Mount McKinley solo. I had been lucky in my previous adventures and I was young, strong and healthy. There was no reason in my mind, albeit foolishly, that I couldn't successfully bag North America's biggest peak. I just had to wait for the threatening weather to subside.

To begin the climb, I needed to take a small Cessna aircraft that would leave me on the glacier at the base of Mount McKinley. I had crashed into the office of Doug Geeting Aviation waiting for my chance to take on this daunting mountain.

I remember ten other people waiting in the small office, all hoping to hit the mountain for backcountry skiing. This type of skiing is where one covers long distances with ups and downs using the same equipment.

The guy sleeping next to me had a bad cold. Sure enough, I caught it.

There was a small window of good weather and I jumped at the opportunity to begin my adventure. I flew to the drop-off zone, and we started by packing the snow where we were going to land. We needed to do three passes, like if we were rock jumping on the water: White, blue, white, blue and hard on the stomach, I experienced.

All that snow and no sign of activity except from a man named Masatoshi Kuriaki, renowned as one of the most accomplished Alaskan winter climbers. He happened to be coming back from a solo ascent of Mount Foraker during the winter/spring.

It is important to note that the native names for Foraker [Sultana] means "wife" of Denali. It is also the second highest peak in North America.

Kuriaki is nicknamed the "Japanese Caribou", a self-applied nickname from a trans-Alaskan walk that happened to coincide with the caribou migration. He has spent more than ten years climbing in the Alaska Range, mostly on the Denali mountain family — mainly solo and predominantly without mishap.

I encourage you to visit his website: http://www.japanesecaribou.com/

After his epic climb of Foraker (I believe he injured his ribs falling into a crevasse), I was the first human Kuriaki had seen in fifty-seven days. His ambition fueled mine and I was determined that it was possible to do a winter ascent of McKinley, as he had. He would surely influence what would happen in the next chapter, as I took on the winter ascent of McKinley.

That said, I began my hike to Camp 1. I was lacking the experience that would allow me to anticipate possible consequences and I didn't consider the effect a cold could have on my very survival. Slowed down by a bad cough, I realized that I was not going to make it to the first designated camp spot.

I decided to pitch a tent along the route as I was the first to be dropped on the mountain and at that point designated Camp 1 was simply a dot on a map. After my departure, two more guys were dropped off, and they were also very speedy. They passed me in a flash. My encounter was very brief. Time to say hello and that was pretty much it. After a few seconds, I was alone all over again. At least, I don't need to break the trail from now on. Throughout the night my illness progressed, and my cough got worse. By morning I was coughing blood.

I was weak, but I refused to listen to my body. I packed up my gear up and continued the climb anyway. After two hours of walking, I was discouraged to realize I had only gained 400 meters of distance. I could still see my previous night's camp! Stubbornly, I kept pushing forward.

Another two hours, and I was only able to push another 400 meters. I was exhausted, but somehow, I found the energy to make camp again

Being so sick and alone, everything became a major effort. I spent one full week covering the distance I would have covered in one day. And there was still no sign of anyone aside the track in the snow. I felt like I was on the moon.

At the base of the ramp leading to Windy Corner I found an igloo someone had built in a previous climbing season. Nothing fancy, more like a hole in the snow. I felt relieved as this meant I didn't need to set up camp that night, and I could get some much-needed rest.

I spent another night alone with my own thoughts.

The following day I saw the "first person" since being dropped at the base of McKinley (the two guys on the route don't count, I had no idea where they were or went). The climber had left base camp the day before and informed me that the rangers were working on preparing for big crowds. In peak season, there were easily several hundred climbers lodged at base camp.

This was good news! I thought if I didn't make it to Windy Corner that day I would return to the igloo and retreat to the base camp. I was disgruntled but not disillusioned by remaining so far from my goal.

Before turning around, I made a food cache. I buried some food in the snow because there was no doubt in my mind that I would be back soon. There was no need to drag it up and down the mountainside in my condition. I marked my stash with garden sticks, wands that mountaineers bring with them to mark their path in the event of a white-out. I would simply take some time to recover at base camp and then begin again. I had given up college and a summer job, giving myself three months to climb this mountain.

It took me three days to make my way back to base camp. The doctor checked me out and ordered me to fly out immediately. He warned that if I didn't, I would more than likely be flown back in a body bag. I complied with the former, but the flight was torturous. I was congested and the pressure in my ears was excruciatingly painful. By the time the plane landed, I could not hear anything. Back in my hometown my doctor prescribed three weeks of antibiotics and eventually my ears unplugged. I was nearly deaf for a month.

During the next couple of weeks, even though I was still feeling beaten up by the mountain, I dreamed about my return. I had no doubt in my mind that I would go back to McKinley. The big question was when.

Chapter 8
Mount McKinley (Denali) Winter (2000)
Strike out!

During my previous expedition early in the season, I had wonderful weather. I took that for granted which probably contributed to me pushing my luck and planning a winter ascent for my next attempt.

And true to my stubborn self, rather than pick the normal route, I decided to take on the West Rib and Orient Express; a much more technical endeavor.

Traveling from east to north-west was becoming expensive. I was flying across country and having to find accommodation. With my desire to explore ever increasing I began searching for an alternative.

For $1500 CAN I found the perfect vehicle that was eventually dubbed the 'Climbing Machine.' I was set for my adventure. Because I would be driving, I felt compelled to tack on an expedition along the way, deciding on Mount Logan, the highest mountain in Canada (5, 959 m) and the second-highest peak in North America, after Mount McKinley. I knew very little about the remote peak, but I was always up for a challenge. I began my research and discussed my plans with people who had climbed it.

I met a guy who attempted the Hummingbird Ridge and he told me that it was not as bad as people say. In fact, he thought that I could probably do it. That was all it took — my mind was set on Hummingbird Ridge!

I figured that it would probably be wise to train all winter in the Canadian Rockies. I needed to find a good partner. I tried to recruit climbers but in vain and, in hindsight, I don't blame them. They were wise enough to be wary of my ambitions. Obviously, I was not smart enough and too young to realize the danger I was putting myself in.

Unlucky within the climber crowd, I began to feel out my friends to see if anyone would be willing to take a year out to come explore the west with me. My friend Sebastien Pilote was ambitious and was dreaming about the outdoors and alpine expeditions. He was going to Mount Logan and was looking for partners.

Since he was a friend, I knew we would get along and he was an incredible athlete. I asked him if he would like to join me and without delay, he agreed. It turned out that Sebastien was the perfect partner. He was a quick learner and never complained on the mountain.

Next, we needed a way to help offset the costs of our trip through various sponsorships and donations. This included raising awareness through fundraising T-shirts and receiving much needed equipment from gracious people and businesses.

A few of the things we received:

-Six pairs of snow shoes from Raquettes GV. We were able to sell each pair for $300 CAN.
-Six ice screws from MEC Calgary. Not very useful for our expedition but most appreciated, especially during our training of ice climbing in the Canadian Rockies. They also bought all our remaining T-shirts which was about fifteen in total.
- Custom-made hats from Pleau. They usually make hats

with fur, but we could not put our climbing helmets on, so they were nice enough to create custom-made hats with no fur.

- The Himalayan foundation lent us a single wall tent, good for serious and light expeditions.

- CHIMO was our clothing provider. I worked for them in the summer at the sea-kayaking school Rivyak and off season in their technical clothing shop. I had spent many hours in the shop, designing the best clothing system, carefully choosing what I would need while climbing over the freezing and treacherous terrain. Our garments were far from the lightweight jackets of today. In the end, it worked out and I strongly believe that, if we had those lightweight jackets, just a small tear and we would be dead, frozen in a block of ice. We did not have the money to buy a fancy jacket. For the price of one jacket, we were dressed from gaiters to mitts and everything in between. We only paid for the sewing, everything else was free.

- Hard shell jackets and bibs, super gaiters, mitts (hard shell and soft), VBL socks, extremely warm underwear (made of fleece "fur", the fur hair was half an inch thick) and special fleece mitts that fitted on top of our regular mitts. All for $700.

- Custom-made backpack from Sub Divo for almost nothing. They made the pack as simple as possible to save weight.

- We didn't carry a radio on the mountain because we had a sponsorship for a satellite phone and solar panels. Back in those days, the satellite phone was still a new thing and the phone was basically the size of a laptop, weighing in at more than fifteen pounds, not including the solar charging system! We were supposed to use it for calling a radio station back home and do a few interviews. At base camp, the phone was not able to get a signal, so we decided to leave it behind in a snow cache, buried and marked with garden stick).

We were still broke, but thanks to the generous support of local people and businesses, we were confident that we could now make the expedition!

First, we headed out for Banff National Park in the prime season of ice climbing. Climbing during the day, camping in the Climbing Machine during the night. We were always able to conveniently find a free parking spot. We also had many ways to sneak into the hotel of Banff and enjoyed a hot tub and warm shower after a long day of ice climbing!

We did few classic lines that include Louise Fall, Cascade, Coire Dubh Integrale, Weeping Wall, Ice Nine and many more. A total of two months filled with pure adventure!

February came, and one day we decided to watch the Super Bowl at Wild Bill's Saloon. We had few beers and I was too drunk to drive the Climbing Machine, so we slept where the van was parked. In the morning, were awakened by the police. They gave us a warning: if they see the Climbing Machine again around town during the next two months, they would be more than happy to give us a ticket for loitering!

That was our cue to hit the road and continue our journey; it was time to leave for Alaska anyway.

We decided from there that we wanted to do an Alpine style expedition. After each day of ascent, we took the day off.

It took a total of fourteen days, but we did not descend to

any of our previous camps and carried everything with us! It was much harder to acclimatize to the altitude, but by the end it became a huge energy saver.

To achieve something of that caliber, we needed to carry the minimum.

Knowing that we would have extremely cold temperatures during the Alaskan winter, I figured that taking off a layer in the morning was probably better than putting it on. Plus, I didn't like to be cold in the morning while getting dressed.

Before my departure, I decided to sell my -40 sleeping bag to Sebastien and brought a five-year-old duvet camp sleeping bag instead. Because it was only a -13 C sleeping bag, I would have to sleep with all my clothes on to keep warm. So, I boarded on the plane wearing all the clothing I would need, with my down jacket and Vapor Barrier socks, in my backpack.

So, for fourteen days in the dead of winter, I trekked Mount McKinley with only one spare pair of socks (for emergency) and the ones I was wearing on the plane that dropped us off on the glacier. For two weeks, I kept on all my clothing (even my bib) continuously, day and night!

In my sleeping bag, I was wearing my hard shell, my down jacket, inner boots and everything in my bivvy bag. In the morning, when we touched the wall of the tent, the condensation from the night before was frozen and fell everywhere. But my sleeping bag was still dry, and I didn't freeze to death!

My trick with the socks almost worked. I did not get frostbite from the cold, however I did get trench foot, from the moisture because of my feet sweating the whole time. As a result, I lost all sensation in my feet for about a year, and I never complained of having ridiculous small rock shoes until the next season, when I got the feeling back in my feet and was not able to even put them on and climb.

I celebrated my twenty-first birthday a few days before our summit push. Sebastien brought me a little present, a chocolate bar. High on the mountain, with world-class view and exposure, made an unforgettable day where I turned to be a real adult with the responsibilities. I'm officially the leader of this endeavor.

We were camped at 5, 000 meters, ready for our summit push, with a possible twelve-to-twenty-hour endeavor to the top. Granted we expected to be on the lower end of that and being stuck on a mountain that big during the night would not be good. It was cold enough during the day, I didn't want to imagine what it would feel like to be exposed to the cold darkness of the night!

We departed our camp at six a.m., well before the sun rose high. We figured if we took a twelve-hour round trip, we would be set to summit at around two p.m. with time to head back down and make it back to camp for six p.m.

Instead of following the well-established route, we decided to cut straight up the mountain. It was very exposed and very steep, but it looked straightforward. Surprisingly, it ended up being a huge short cut!

The only downfall was that we did not anticipate how big of a shortcut it would be. In only roughly four hours, we were standing on the summit plateau Football Field at 5, 880 meters. On a regular climb, this would be great news. But on this climb, the sun had not even risen, which meant that it was excruciatingly cold. In fact, it was so cold that we could not go any further!

We didn't summit that day, but we came close. We both

had the energy, we were still feeling strong and we were ahead of schedule, but it was simply too cold to continue. There was no other reason to turn around than the frigid temperature.

We retreated and in one hour we were back at the tent. That's when we felt the ground shaking. I jumped outside to witness the most extraordinary mountain scene: giant avalanches were coming down on every mountain flank. Some debris was even sliding down where we were climbing less than an hour ago. It was shocking and enlightening. That was the closest call in my life. All that fresh debris waiting to fall made it simply unsafe to keep going. Let say that we were very small prior the incident. We were even smaller after. I need to admit; it scared the crap out of us. An earthquake had shaken the ground and the epicenter was fearfully close to McKinley.

So why we didn't go for the summit a second time? As two young guys (eighteen and twenty-one years old), Sebastien and I were proud to have made it as far as we did on the climb. However, after the immense avalanche we had just witnessed, we were too scared to continue.

I was slowly realizing that I was the one with the most experience and began to understand that I may be responsible if something were to happen to Sebastien. The responsibility weighed on me and I didn't want anything to happen to him. I was beginning to think like a guide.

From my cross-country skiing days, through to my reckless years of climbing, I was learning how important it was to tackle my sport with more experience and mindfulness.

It was time to drive away in the Climbing Machine, where I would make my new base camp in Whitehorse!

Chapter 9
Yukon (2000)
Peanut butter!

My van had become my home and Whitehorse, Yukon became my base camp. Plus, I finally had a day off!

The Climbing Machine had a battery problem that needed to be fixed before the long trip back to Canmore. Every time my battery was connected while the van was running, the battery would overcharge and boil over. The regulator was faulty. It was not an expensive problem, but every dollar counts when you are a climbing bum. I had managed the problem for five months by disconnecting my battery while it was running and connecting it again to start the van. All this just to save ten bucks.

I figured it was time to invest so I planned a stop at the auto parts store. First, I needed to fill up my gas tank.

I pulled into the gas station, filled up my van and went in to pay. I came out to see smoke billowing out of my window. I mean a lot! I ran inside the gas station and I yelled in my terrible English, "My home is on fire! My home is on fire!"

The manager ran out with a fire extinguisher. We pushed the van and the burning flames away from the pumps. Then we opened the back door and looked inside. The manager was standing there just watching the van burn down. Compelled into action I pushed him inside and he finally began to spray the inside of the Climbing Machine with the extinguisher.

Eventually, two fire trucks drove up. They couldn't figure out what had caused to fire. All I knew was the fire had wreaked havoc on the back of my van and my toilet was melted.

I was homeless for a week. The yellow powder from the fire extinguisher was all over everywhere. Even so, I worked hard to get the Climbing Machine cleaned up and ready to go.

Eventually, I was on the road again and ended up on an old remote Alaskan highway heading for Canmore. It was a beautiful evening for a drive. I stopped for gas, and as I filled up the van I began to reflect on the wonderful time I had had up North and the wonderful people I had met. I would really miss the Yukon and I remember saying to myself that I would be back.

Sadly, I have never had the opportunity.

As I pumped my gas, I continued to reflect on my climbing adventures. Then, I felt a flow of air from the van accompanied by a loud 'VOMG' noise. Then I witnessed an explosion.

What was going on? I immediately opened the back door of the van. I could see a rusty pipe with some holes and I assumed that must be my filler tube. Right beside it sat the fridge. I understood immediately what had happened: warm day plus gas station plus old van.

While pumping gas, the vapors had escaped from the rusty holes and collected behind my counter. This had not been a problem in the winter as the cold air seemed to contain the vapors and prevent them from building up to dangerous levels. The pilot light from my fridge was just waiting for enough gas vapors to collect before igniting the unsuspectingly home-built bomb. This time I was lucky enough to not cause another fire!

During that same summer a van of the very same make, model and year had made the news. It had started on fire at the pump as well.

Unlike mine it blew the whole station up. Cause of the fire: unknown.

I'm pretty sure I know how it happened, and I felt very lucky to have figured out the problem without having had a bigger catastrophe and I decide to keep it to myself. I was the proud owner of a 1976 Dodge Craftsman and I was just slightly luckier than those poor guys. I didn't want to cause any trouble.

It had turned to spring just after the expedition on McKinley. Sebastien and I were looking forward to Logan but it was too early in the season to climb it. We set up a base camp in Whitehorse and planned to climb Mount Logan via the Hummingbird Ridge.

In hindsight I am very glad we never did get a shot at that endeavor as I don't believe it would have gone as well as my previous risky ambitions. I had become seasoned enough to know it was way above our experience level. I don't believe we would have survived such an overestimation of our abilities. At least we weren't ignorant enough to go when the mountain wasn't in seasonal condition.

We prepared for a good two months' delay before attacking Mount Logan. Peanut butter was the only food we were able to afford that was at all filling for two active young men. Peanut butter for breakfast, peanut butter for lunch and peanut butter for dinner. I decided that I needed to find some work.

I got myself an interview at the Pizza Hut for a kitchen position. The supervisor was very impressed by my resume. Instead of giving me the kitchen position she offered me a job as a server. Maybe she thought I had a cute accent. My first shift was the next morning. I was not convinced that I was the best to communicate well with guests. It turned out I was right. After my first table, I was demoted to folding pizza boxes. On my second shift, I was fired.

I did find a new job shortly after and finally I got a break from peanut butter. This time my job was in French. Because of the high demand for French speakers I was hired to conduct surveys over the phone to Quebecers. I was getting paid more than my co-workers who were unilingual English.

Around that same time Sebastien had had enough of the dedicated climber lifestyle of base camps in the Climbing Machine and peanut butter and decided to return in Quebec. He told me that he would return for Logan but, deep down, I knew that he would not return. By that time, I knew that it wasn't smart to venture out alone on a big mountain like Logan.

Climbing with Sebastian was an adventure, but unfortunately, McKinley was to be our only expedition together. Our paths diverged: he moved on to the RCMP and I ventured off to my training to become a guide. We never did get the chance to plan another climb together.

I had attempted six peaks over 5, 000 meter plus four peaks over 6, 000 meter and I just turned twenty-one years old. I was getting arrogant and I felt that the world was mine for the taking. But I would be knocked down a notch or two.

I started to do research on the Association of Canadian Mountain Guides at the Whitehorse public library. The registration was already full for the alpine program and there was a waiting list. I decided to put myself on that list. I needed to fill out the application in English, so I used that library's Internet to apply and my cellphone as my contact number.

A few weeks later I got a phone call from the ACMG headquarters.

"Sir, you cannot jump directly to the Alpine program," the man on the other end of the line explained. "You need to do the Rock program first and we have had somebody that drop out this morning. Do you want that spot?"

"I'm not a rock climber. I'm a mountain climber. I don't need the Rock, what I want is to be an Alpine Guide," I replied.

"You cannot do that. You do the Rock first and then the Alpine. Do you want the spot or not? The course is next month."

"I guess so. Yes," I conceded.

I got off the phone and I looked at the requirements — 5.11a (6b+) on traditional. On trad routes, you must place your own protection which you carry up with you as opposed to sport climbing, where you use gear mounted into the rock face. This requirement was much more difficult than I had anticipated.

On my résumé my hardest climb was only 5.9 (5b), so I wondered why they had offered me the spot and assumed it was my extensive alpine experience. I guess it was not every day that you would come across a kid of twenty-one with such an impressive list of accomplishments and had lived to tell about it.

Another major challenge to face. I would have to get up to those climbing grades, but I would need to go somewhere where there was some real climbing to do. Destination: Bow Valley.

Chapter 10
There's a Monster in the Climbing Machine (2000)

I was walking in Banff and I recognize a familiar face. It's Sebastien Fortin, another friend with the same first name as my previous climbing partner.

He is an older friend from back home. We shared the same passion for the mountain. (I think we met while kayaking on a river, but I could be wrong.)

I asked him what he was doing out west and he told me that he and some friends had made the trip all the way from Quebec to climb Mount Athabasca. Then they asked if I would like to join the four of them: Sebastien and his wife Magalie, J. F. Cantin and a French guy they had met up with. Their objective was the north face, a grade III, 5.4 (4a). I jumped at the chance to get out and decided to tag along.

Once it is in your blood you must find a place to explore and there is no other place in the world like the Rockies!

Jacynthe, my future wife, and her friend were traveling with me as they had just wrapped up an all-woman's mountain bike expedition. Since I would be gone two days for Mount Athabasca, I offered them the Climbing Machine and told them where they could park for the night for free.

By two a.m. it was snowing, and the weather was not good at all. We were getting snowed in at our little bivouac.

Thankfully by seven the weather had improved significantly. My friends decided on a late start and I followed along.

Our group was slow to prepare in the morning but eventually we get moving. We accomplished the approach quickly and then began the actual climb. Early on, my partner, who was equipped with one mountaineer ice axe and one proper ice axe, showed signs of trouble on the climb.

I watched as the other team was also having difficulty with their anchors.

The French guy had forgotten his sunscreen. He was wearing a tight balaclava and wearing sunglasses, so the only skin exposed were his cheeks and forehead. Because of this, he ended up burning his face in a perfect circle, except for around the eyes. He had a souvenir for many days of his epic climb!

It was eight o'clock at night and we were at the rock band. Snowy weather had moved in. I had taken virtual pictures of the way down to try to ensure that we could make it back in the dark safely.

I asked who was leading the mixed part and everyone looks back at me as though it was not a real question.

"Of course, it's you," they told me.

I took the lead and ended up just below the summit. I looked for an anchor and prepared to bring the next person up behind me.

I yelled "On belay!" and listened for someone's signal that they were beginning up the pitch. I listened and heard nothing. I don't feel any movement on the rope. Why weren't they moving? There was no slack in the rope and I was bearing a lot of weight on my feet.

After one hour, nothing was happening. I was frustrated

but had no option but to wait. Finally, I saw someone coming up on the rope. I realized that he was climbing up the rope with prusik knots and not the route itself. That explained why the rope was not moving, the constant load and lots of weight on my belay. He explained that they had all decided to ascend the route via the rope I had just fixed and give up on the climb itself.

Eventually we were descending, but we were in a total white-out. The group wanted to spend the night near the summit. I was the black sheep of the group who didn't want to stop. Maybe, after all, it was the decision to take but when I have something in mind, it's hard to convince me otherwise.

We had no sleeping gear except a tarp for the group. I said, "No thank you, I'm not going to freeze to death in a snowbank." Good thing it was still close to the summer equinox when the night's darkness is only a few hours long.

I pushed for heading down the mountain and I was sure I could find my way. I was on the same mountain four months ago with Sebastien Pilot, so the terrain was familiar. Luckily, I came through and we were back at the car twenty-four hours after we left our bivouac. It was frustrating that we had taken so long to climb something I could have done in a matter of hours. It ended safely at least but it was less than the enjoyable quick trip I was hoping to tag onto.

While I was on my adventure, the girls and the Climbing Machine had one of their own.

They found the place I had suggested to park and bunkered down to sleep. In the middle of the night one woman woke up and started to scream. The other jumped up and joined in. There was something big moving inside the van! Jacynthe grabbed a flashlight and pointed it in the direction of the movement. Two small green eyes glowed in the dark back at them and they screamed even more. Jacynthe's partner grabbed the broom and begins flailing it around the entire van following the shining eyes. Finally, it seemed as if they had scared off the unwanted visitor. Terrified they scarcely slept for the rest of the night, worried that their intruder may return.

They prepared for bed the second night but kept a fire alarm handy to set off in case of the animal's return, hoping the noise would permanently dissuade him from choosing their bed as his own. They managed to fall asleep. Again, Jacynthe woke up in the middle of the night to something on her sleeping bag and it was big and it was heavy.

When she realized it was there, she began screaming and set off the alarm. It worked, and the animal disappeared. Jacynthe drifted off but her partner could not. It was one of those very long wakeful nights. Her partner felt a big weight move on to her sleeping bag. She screamed and kicked at the intruder. Jass set off the alarm. I wasn't until dawn was approaching that the woman could relax enough to get a bit of shut-eye.

We later figured out that a pine marten was venturing in via my melted toilet. The dump hole was a perfect hallway up into the toilet and the three-inch melted hole served as the doorway into a warm and food-stocked cave; the perfect find for any adventurous animal.

I reunited with Jacynthe and turned my attention to rock climbing. I had to become a proficient rock climber before I began my rock-guiding course. I managed to form a list of the potential routes they would be climbing in the course the following week. No more peanut butter because I needed to slim down. Jacynthe and I were on a mission to climb all the routes repeatedly until I could climb them smoothly.

I was not a 5.11 (6b+) climber, but I was determined to make them believe I was. At first it was ugly as I struggled my way up the difficult climbs. Good thing the instructors never had the chance to observe my first attempts, as I was not fooling anyone. It wasn't fun, but I took it like it was work. Messy labor, I was bleeding from both my knees. I was simply not experienced enough. My belay slave was not complaining too much except for when I was hanging for too long.

I climbed and climbed until I had the list of climbs dialed.

I was completely over my head in the course. Everything was a challenge. The techniques and course work were one thing, but I still spoke fairly broken English and that made keeping up all the more difficult.

I did the climbing screening by sticking to my list and nobody seemed to notice that I was not a competent rock climber. The course was being held in the Rockies and the multi-pitch routes on limestone had much more of an alpine feel. I found the routes almost familiar. If it had been in Squamish on the smooth pumpy granite, I don't think I would have fared quite so well.

I was relieved to find I was not the only one from Quebec. I got to know Francois Roy, a very strong, recognized climbing pioneer from the French province. We partnered up after the course and achieved a beautiful first ascent. We became kindred spirits and I admired his push on those big climbs. We claimed the first ascent of the routes Exacto and the test piece 'The Jour Le Plus Long' on the north-east face of Wind Tower, ~550 meters, 5.11 or 5.10d (6b+ or 6b). Raphael Slawinski, a well-known climber within the climbing community commented on it in his blog:

"This outstanding route was established on the summer solstice in 2000 by two Quebecois climbers, Remy Bernier and Francois Roy, in just about the best style possible: on-sight and hammerless. Rolando Garibotti and I made the second ascent in 2003 and added a two-pitch variation, making for easier but more consistent climbing. I hope that others will respect the pure style in which the route was put up and leave their hammers behind when enjoying one of the finest long routes the Front Ranges have to offer."

Then, I needed to grow up and take a real job, but before, I needed to do a quick 'pit stop' in Quebec.

Chapter 11
The Climbing Machine is dying (2000)

After two weeks of climbing with Francois, the Climbing Machine broke down again. I was driving when suddenly it had no brakes. To the Chrysler dealership in Canmore I went. My master cylinder was faulty. It should have been an easy fix, putting the part in and bleeding the brakes — one hour maximum.

But two weeks later, I was still sleeping in the back-parking lot of the dealership. Sixteen hours of labor later, they fixed the Climbing Machine. Time to pay and I didn't have the fifteen hundred dollars for the bill. I met with the owner and he wanted me to work for him for $6/hr. I refused, saying that I am worth at least $8/hr. He conceded, and he is willing to cut the bill of the repair by half. I became the new wash boy and shuttle driver and began work the next morning.

I climbed a lot in anticipation for the Assistant Rock Guide exam but washing cars and climbing did not pair well. I developed tendonitis in my shoulder which hindered my ability to climb. A few months later I was promoted to apprentice automotive technician and decided to make Canmore my hometown. I planned my trip back to Quebec in the Climbing Machine, where I would pick up my belongings and move to Alberta.

By the last ten kilometers the Climbing Machine was overheating. It was too hilly to get to my home in St-Feréol-Les-Neiges, so I called CAA (AMA). The tow-truck driver was worried that we would not clear the electrical wires, so he called another truck to escort me home. With the bright yellow lights of the two trucks traveling slowly at ten km/h, the last stretch of country hills was long, but eventually, the boy was back in town!

I wasn't going to give up on the beast. I replaced the radiator in the Climbing Machine and stripped the inside, so it functioned more like a cargo van. I filled it up and hit the road for the 4, 000-kilometer drive west.

After this, I figured that it was about time to trade in the Climbing Machine for a brand-new car. Also, I thought, I should probably cut this 'hippy hair' and become an adult!

Chapter 12
It's on!

I arrived in Canmore without incident. I cut off my long hair, moved into an apartment, found a brand-new car and bought an engagement ring. It was Christmas 2000 when I gave Jacynthe the ring. She was silent for two weeks before she finally accepted my proposal.

It would be five more years before we would marry. Jacynthe still lived in Quebec and was finishing her physiotherapy diploma at the University.

This incident took place in the summer of 2001. Jass was spending her summer in Canmore. The refrigerator was broken, and the laundry needed to be done. Since she was only working half days at Lake Louise, Jass decided to take care of it. She was going to take the car, clean out the fridge and take the food to a friend, and do the laundry at the laundromat. I told her that she might as well take my wallet.

Anyway, we were supposed to arrive from work at the same time. I was home, but there was no Jass. Three hours later (no food, no clothes, no car and no wallet) I decided to go look in the street where I saw my car parked in front. She had gone for a beer after work at the neighborhood pub. One beer turned into many and she completely forgot about me.

I was choked! So, I took my wallet, my keys and my car. I drove to get my frustration out and ended up in Exshaw on a gravel parking lot about twenty-five meters from the edge of the forest.

I saw something moving and got out of the car. I walked closer to find out what it was. At eight feet a grizzly bear jumped in front of me and got up on his two back legs. I really don't know if there were cubs around but most likely there were. My car was twenty-five meters away, the door was open, and the keys were in the ignition. I'm a good sprinter so I decided to outrun the grizzly. I got to the car first and I spun my wheels in the gravel parking lot. Rocks were flying toward the grizzly. A huge cloud of dust left the grizzly all gray and old looking.

Remy: Win, grizzly: Lost!

It was a close one, but it wasn't my time to go yet! This made me realize the weight of what I considered important in my life. I had moved six times in two years, but now, it was time to settle down with Jacynthe. She joined me for my last move to Calgary. There were northern lights in the sky that night.

In 2003 I wanted to get thinner for my full rock exam, which I did end up passing. I headed to Squamish where the climbing would help me work on my strength. I always ran a bit from time to time but never seriously. I had, however, been dragging myself up giant mountains for years so I decided to register for the Stampede Road Race marathon. I went for a two-week climbing trip just before the race so I did very little running and a whole lot of climbing. I ran the race without any real training. I was proud to finish third in my age group, in three and a half hours!

In 2004 I had a chance to work overseas, in Switzerland, at the second most expensive school on the planet. It sounded like a great opportunity. I was hired for my outdoor skills and experience. I went to feel it out with tentative plans to have Jacynthe join me eventually. The position was an internship which meant I was staying on campus always surrounded by students.

One of the many activities that I participated in was at the ski station Argentière, near Chamonix, France. I was shadowing the good friend that had referred me for the job. There was more than thirty centimeters of fresh snow. I was so excited to go, but the kids not so much. We managed to coerce the students onto the chairlift. After two minutes of outdoor adventure all the kids were on the ground, playing dead and forming a strike.

We did only one run that day, only a couple turns in knee-deep snow. I couldn't understand their lack of enthusiasm and I was disappointed in how it all played out. Undeterred, we organized a dream trip of heli-skiing one weekend. Again, I was more excited than any student on the trip. We had to cancel because they all wanted to sleep in that Saturday.

Shocked and amazed by the lack of appreciation the students had for their amazing opportunities, I packed my gear and went straight back to Canada.

Finding myself back home with no job I decided to challenge the final two exams for my automotive technician certification. The last year was on automatic transmissions. It was putting my brain to sleep.

The first exam was complex compared to the second one, which focused on the material learned over the four years. By passing that last exam, technicians get a special certification called Red Seal. Red Seal recipients have the choice to work nationwide. If you failed, you were only allowed to work in Alberta. Unsure of where I would be in the future — Alberta or Quebec — I wanted a good score on that final test. The wait was awful, but I was relieved to finally get news that I had passed.

As luck would have it, if you were to ask me the most basic of questions today, I would not even know the answer!

Chapter 13
Faster… I don't like Sleeping in the cold Any more!

I was with my good friend Tom Wolfe. We were at the Deville rappels on the Bugaboo to Rogers Pass Ski Traverse. A vertical cliff of 150 meters was at our feet. We brought minimal gear to save weight during the traverse. In fact, we only brought thirty-five meters of rope, and we needed sixty meters to do the rappels. But we left out the remaining twenty-five meters for a reason: it would have significantly increased the weight of our already big load.

 We came to an agreement to do the rappels on a single strand, on a blocking knot and to retrieve the rope with all the pieces of rope we could find tied together. We tied every bit of cord, tat and sling (including cutting my double length sling that was sewn in a loop) to be able to make the pulls. We salvaged two five-meter pieces of cord from one of the stations, which made the raps more doable. I think we tied about ten knots all together.

 My partner went first for the last rappel. He had to build a two-piton anchor as he didn't traverse far enough into the chimney. Good thing we had some rock gear with us because, we would never have made it safely to the ground.

 Our plan worked. It was exciting, and I loved it! I would jump at the chance to experience that adventure all over again if I could.

The Bugs to Rogers was my first ski traverse period. It was also my longest. In total the trip covers 120 kilometers of wilderness and gains nearly 10, 000 meters. Crossing the Purcell and Selkirk Mountains in British Columbia, the traverse travels through the jagged granite spires of the Bugaboos as it works its way north through the large connected path of glaciers and summits. We completed the trip in seven days and six nights in late April, 2005.

Side note: I switched from telemarking to alpine touring in 2005 because it was a more efficient way of guiding.

Chapter 14
Training mode!

This is a recollection of my mountaineering trips with Jesse DeMontigny done in the summer 2005

We were going to attempt the complete traverse of the famous Three Sisters. These mountains are close to Canmore and see only a few ascents every year. In fact, less than five climbers have ventured further than the first peak. The complete traverse has been done and repeated, but at the time it was still waiting for a third ascent.

We sprinted over the first peak and were on target to complete the traverse in a day. We were high on the Second Sister, which is the crux of the climb. Having completed that part of the climb, we figured we could walk/scramble over the third objective.

Unfortunately, we were given a bad description of the route. After having read the directions over and over, it was Jesse's turn to take the lead. After much deliberation, we decided that Jesse would go left. This was considered "no man's land." After more than one hour, Jesse belayed me up. I've seen lots of anchors in my life, but that one was probably the worst!

We were lost, fifty meters to the left of where we needed to be and had only one marginal red Camelot as an anchor.

With the abyss at the edge, not much higher than our original anchor, it would not be possible to retreat other than where we came from. Thankfully, the climbing was easy at this point, because I doubted the Camelot would hold a fall.

Going back was not as easy! I had no other choice than leaving my Camelot behind. We traversed back without putting our full weight on the questionable anchor. Back to safety, we pulled on one side of the rope, but it wasn't moving. At that point, Jesse suggested calling a helicopter rescue.

From where we were, I could see our house and I knew that Jass has been looking all day at the Three Sisters. I could just imagine her seeing the helicopter and thinking the worst. I couldn't bear the thought of her worrying, so I told Jesse, "I will go up the rope with prusik knots and make the rope free again".

I stood by our unreliable anchor, praying for it to hold once more. I was terrified: no words could describe the precariousness of the situation. We did a bunch of rappels to escape and had to leave cordelettes and two or three expensive Camelots on the wall, but we made it back home safely, and well before dinner.

That same year we did another successful trip together; this time we took on the Bugaboo range. In two days of stunning weather, we climbed Snowpatch Spire, the northeast face of Bugaboo Spire and the easy route of Pigeon Spire.

We were back on Monday morning guiding rock climbing with the British cadets.

Later, we made the traverse of the Swiss Peaks and Mount Tupper in Rogers pass. Again, it was a nice outing for the weekend.

I decided to save the best (or worst, depending on your viewpoint) adventure Jesse and I did, for the last: the traverse of the Ten Peaks near Lake Louise. Again, this was just over one weekend.

You're probably wondering "how come big objective during the weekend?" Jesse and I had summer jobs, Monday to Friday, guiding rock climbing with the British cadets, all summer long. The weekends were used to polish our climbing resume, as we were planning to register for the Alpine Guide Program. We were looking forward to heading to a place where the food would be good, and the nights would be warm!

Believe me, if this was just for fun, I would rather go sport climbing.

Chapter 15
The big day, more Skiing and Climbing.

The day finally arrived for my wedding to Jacynthe. We had a lovely civil ceremony on October 15th, 2005 in Quebec. It was important for us to return home to share that moment with our families. Seeing everyone gathered for our special day was heart-warming. My wife was a princess. We enjoyed the food along with the tam-tam band that I had hired. They were not at all a serious wedding band, but they created a lively atmosphere. I was so impressed by Jacynthe's planning, and the day was by far the most beautiful and enjoyable of my entire life.

Winter of 2006 was the last chance to work on my skiing resume.

My good friend James Madden and I had met at the Campbell Icefield. I was the custodian of the Campbell Icefield Chalet located in the west slopes of the Canadian Rocky Mountains near Golden, British Columbia. The Chalet was classified as a backcountry hut, and it was only accessible by helicopter. The guests would come in for a week at the time. James' group happened to be my first clients of the year. After hanging out for one week with the guy, I knew he was the ideal partner for a major ski traverse.

Soon after, we chose to ski the Gold Range traverse near Revelstoke, British Columbia.

The last half of the trip had been done before but not the first half. The linkage of the two parts covered the complete range from Mt Odin to Three Valley Gap. The linkup covered about 120 kilometers and the first part was kicking our butt as it is definitely for skiers with good ability due to the difficulty of very steep skiing with heavy loads.

We were carrying food for ten days, and the trip took a total of six days and five nights.

The trip was not recommended if there was even a slight chance of an avalanche. There was no risk at the beginning of the trip, but later on was another story: There were slides all around us! We were at a lower elevation than we had started the adventure but all the challenging terrain that we had to navigate was behind us. We did the traverse in March 2006, the last winter before my stroke.

We did two other trips together that year in April and really tried to stretch the ski season, but the elements had the final word. It was time to stop for the season.

Chapter 16
Forced to play the hero!

Little did I know that the summer of 2006 would be the last year of climbing before I had my stroke.

I was completely focused on training for my assistant Alpine exam. I was alpine climbing at every opportunity. I had partnered with my friend Jesse Demontigny and we had been doing some serious missions.

Also, during that time a friend of mine came for a visit. He was complaining that the Rockies only had a few decent grade VI routes. Woo! I was excited and prepared to show him and his girlfriend the Canadian Rockies that I had grown to know and love.

I decided to see how they would enjoy the East Ridge of Mount Temple first. We were high on Mount Temple with the summit at striking distance. The girlfriend was doing fine but my friend was not! He was feeling dizzy and began to become incoherent. The summit is only fifteen minutes away but he couldn't continue. I had no choice but to call for a rescue on my radio.

Ten minutes later Parks Canada rescue wardens were there and within half an hour we were carried out by helicopter. Because they couldn't land, we were slung underneath the helicopter by a long rope. The view of Mount Temple from that perspective was amazing! After a quick assessment of my friend, it was concluded that he had started to experience altitude sickness. The wardens assured me that radioing in was the right call to have made.

The following weekend, after my friend had recovered, we decided to give the Rockies another go. We bivouacked the night before we tackled Mount Stanley by its north face. I had chosen the grade III route Kahl. We had a lovely ascent and descent. As we were just about to leave the glacier, I turned to look one more time at this magnificent mountain but, instead, I watched a man fall from the mountain.

A party of two that had been climbing a couple hours behind us was near the summit when one fell off into a gully system, falling more than 400 meters.

I contacted the rescue wardens right away and initiated a rescue mission. I parked my two friends in a safe spot and started for the injured climber. When I got to him one artery was punctured. A large flow of blood was escaping his body, timed to the beat of his heart, and it was scarily decreasing with every beat.

I stopped the deadly bleeding with whatever I had on hand. I can't even recall what it was, but the important thing was I had stopped it. A couple minutes later the helicopter came with the same rescuer as the week before. For the second time in a week I was slung underneath a helicopter for a rescue. I saved a man's life that day and the victim recovered fully.

I was given a medal of honor by the Association of Canadian Mountain Guides (ACMG) for my response. Sometimes I still think about him climbing out there, as I spend my life in a chair dreaming of those days.

I thought I had had my fair share of bad luck with two

helicopter rescues back to back. Little did I know that in a matter of weeks I would be travelling on those same helicopters and not as a rescuer.

The following weekend, I continued training for my guide exam with some friends in Rogers Pass. We stopped for a breather in a huge boulder field. We watched as a guy was jumping from boulder to boulder. Unexpectedly he dislodged a big boulder and it began to roll, crashing right towards us. I had just enough time to get out of the way but one of my friends was not so lucky. The boulder rolled over his hand crushing muscles, tendons and nerves. His hand was not pinned so we managed to get him out of the pass and to the hospital without calling for a rescue.

Three rescues in three weekends. Up until now I had managed to explore the wild outdoors without the reality of the dangers so blatantly staring me in the face. After having been witness to and involved in only a few of the threats that await anyone who ventures off into the back country, I wasn't sure I was up for the responsibility. Maybe I didn't want to be a guide any more. Maybe I should just drop out the Assistant Alpine Guide exam.

Before I made any hasty decisions, I took some time to reflect on my experiences. I realized the value in each journey and knew that, in the end, they would make me a better guide. In a month I was back in the mountains where I belonged, and I completed my exam.

Chapter 17
My Sweetie

After the exam, I spent some quality time with my wife, and we finally went on our honeymoon.

Nothing too fancy, just a simple road trip and camping. We started with Penticton, BC but our main objective was California and Nevada. We planned to finally hit the City of Lights. Most tourists visit the Las Vegas. Not us — we planned to climb in Red Rock and camp on the edge of the city.

Total vacation time: one month! Just in time to get back home and enjoy my last three days as an able-bodied person.

We saw the legendary Yosemite, the Mecca of rock climbing. Unfortunately, there was no campsite available in the entire valley. After taking few pictures with the famous Nose of El Capitan in the background, we continued our trip to the High Sierra and Bishop. We picked Bishop for its incredible sport climbing and a campsite was not an issue. In fact, we were surprised to see only few people.

Before heading to Las Vegas, we tackled the High Sierra. This region is the home of Mount Whitney, the highest summit in the USA in the lower 48, with its summit rising to 4, 421 meters. It was important for me to climb that mountain. It would become a great memory for me, especially after my stroke, which would hit me just two weeks later.

We did the approach in a day. The weather was simply blue bird with not even a trace of cloud. *Blue bird* means very hot for us Albertans. Hiking with the massive granite spires made all the sweat worth it. I don't think I have ever done an approach with so many things to see!

At the base camp we socialized with two Americans. Tomorrow they were going to climb Whitney by the East Face while we were going for the East Buttress. It was a more direct line and a little more difficult than the East Face Route; it also offered technical climbing at high elevation on rock-solid granite. Quite different than our limestone in the Bow Valley.

We were up before everybody including the two Americans. We were the first on the rock, but it was a good thing we set the alarm for six o'clock. The two Americans hit the rock two hours later. By the time they started, we were already high on the giant peak. We were climbing very fast, they weren't. I was a fresh assistant alpine guide. I had my systems dialed and my "client" was very fast too!

Two pitches from the top, it started snowing. By the time we reached the top, the flakes were as thick as small marbles and it was a complete blizzard. We went down by the scrambling route called "the Mountaineers' Route." We were back at camp one hour later. We ran on the way down. The rocks were already covered with snow when we reached the safety of our camp.

It was nine p.m. and there was no sign of the Americans. I got into my sleeping bag, a little bit worried. The night passed and, in the morning, we woke up with thirty centimeters of snow on our shelter. Still no sign of the Americans. We packed up everything and started to trace back our way to the car.

At the car park we recognized their vehicle right away because they signed in at the trailhead and had left their plate number beside their names. I wrote a note and placed it on their windshield. The note said that we were worried and to drop me a line by email when they returned to safety.

A couple of days later, I received an email from them. The couple was able to reach the top and found refuge in an old meteorological structure at the top. When they woke up, the snow was over knee-deep.

They decided to hike down the other side of the mountain on the Cottonwood trail leaving their camp behind. They hiked the eighteen kilometer of the Cottonwood trail the day after their epic climb and had slept in their car. It was the second night in a row without sleeping gear. The following day they hiked to the other side of the mountain and finally slept in their sleeping bags. Hiking back on the third day they were able to rescue the rest of their gear and head home. It was finally over; their long weekend outing (usually three days) turned out to be almost a week long (five days).

It was only possible to avoid the storm with a fast partner. Jacynthe and I made a very good team. We worked together on climbing from the early days in Quebec. We pushed each other to our limits. Me, climbing slightly harder, she always challenged me to push my limit on harder routes. Consequently, she needed always to push her own limits to retrieve all the gear (job of the second climber).

I was the leader and she was climbing with a top rope.

The last two years she wanted to be a leader so we both had our projects and we were cleaning the routes on the way down. Our favorite type of climbing was sport. We did a few multi-pitch gear climbs like the one at the beginning of this chapter. Sport climbing was much harder, which in turn gave us the ability to climb faster on easier terrain.

We were both very competitive and enjoyed doing the same sports. As an ex-alpine skier, she was kicking my ass at the resort. Not so much in backcountry, but she was still way better than me. Cross-country skiing was my forte, and we both enjoyed mountain biking. We also planned an expedition in Aconcagua.

Jass has always been the kind of lady who doesn't mind getting dirty. For example: as a teen she worked in a mine in northern Quebec as a laborer/mechanic during the summer.

When she went caving, she was not afraid to crawl on all fours and get dirty. I loved that she was bold and unafraid to take on new adventures.

At home we were also the Dream Team. I seem to recall only one actual fight in the eight years that Jass and I were together. Unfortunately, it would be *after* my stroke that we would experience a major life-changing hurdle. We'll touch on that later, as this would be another key turning point in our lives.

That said; I'm more fortunate than most people. Even after all the battles I fought and will fight I'm so fortunate to still be alive!

Chapter 18
Remy Bernier, Mountaineer by Chic Scott

Remy is a free spirit and would not fit into the mold. He had no fear of doing things differently, Jean Francois Monette.

Remy and Jean Francois Monette met in high school and shared many adventures together, including several excursions to the Adirondack Mountains of New York State. According to Jean Francois, Remy always had a plan and once he had his plan there was no stopping him. He was strong, determined and had perseverance.

But it didn't take long for Remy to realize that he needed bigger mountains to realize his dreams. Mountains like Aconcagua in Argentina and Denali (Mount McKinley) in Alaska. Amazingly Remy, at the age of twenty-one, almost climbed Denali in winter. It was a bold and dangerous undertaking, but Remy and his companion very nearly succeeded.

Remy couldn't stay in the same place very long and had to keep moving. And it was in western Canada where Remy found his mountains and a community of climbers where he fitted in. He began his quest to become a licensed mountain guide and met Tom Wolfe at the Assistant Rock Guide exam in 2001. Remy was twenty-two years old and could barely speak English. Despite his lack of experience and his language difficulties he took the exam seriously and did well.

Tom remembers that Remy had to teach a session on

threading the rope in the anchor (a technique used to retrieve all the gear). He fabricated a plywood board with two sets of climbing anchors, one with rappel rings and one with hangers. He spent hours thinking it through and had notes to help him remember. He was hard to understand but Remy was determined to be a guide.

Another good friend of Remy is Jesse De Montigny. For several years they worked together on the rock-climbing program at the Cadet Camp. "Remy was determined and focused and could be serious too. He was really dedicated and wanted to do a good job."

Remy and Tom did the Bugaboos to Rogers Pass Ski Traverse in April 2005. As they drove to the start of the tour Remy confided to Tom that he had never done any type of ski traverse before. The traverse took them a week and they had excellent conditions allowing them to do all the high and difficult variants. The next year he was accepted into the ski guide program. According to Tom, "Remy was a good skier, a real natural athlete."

Jesse and Remy had some good adventures together. In the Bugaboos they climbed Snowpatch and Pigeon Spires in a day. In the Rockies they did the traverse of the Ten Peaks from Wenkchemna Pass to the Perren route, a long and difficult climb on loose rock.

According to Jesse, "Remy was very motivated. He was always busy doing something, working on his vehicle or renovating the house. Over the years he lived his dream with very little money."

In Canmore Remy had found a home and a career. Guiding was a way for Remy to live his passion. He received his rock guide license in 2003 and 2006 passed his assistant alpine guide exam. He was well on his way to becoming a mountain guide, a dream he cherished.

Chapter 19
Foothills Hospital (2006–2007)
If you don't eat Everything, you won't get Dessert!

For Christmas 2006, I planned to leave the hospital for a few days to spend time with my family, and to visit at a friend's house. To prepare, my occupational therapist taught Jacynthe how to transfer me into a vehicle. The first try wasn't smooth, and it certainly wasn't pretty, but my OT knew that I was tougher than I looked and could handle being thrown around a bit. With that, she gave us the authorization to head out. Anyone else may have had to have spent Christmas in the hospital.

My parents took a plane all the way from Quebec just for me, so I would not have to spend Christmas alone. They stayed for two weeks, following me every day at my rehab, simply to spend time with me.

Without them, it would have been much more difficult to go through those hard times. At the time, I wanted to tell them how much I appreciated them. The only problem was that I could not speak or write. I miss my parents. They both passed away from cancer.

I guess I will have to wait until I'm old to see if I have good genes or not! I mean, with my AVM being undetected when I was born, I've already won the lottery (note my sarcasm). What will life throw at me next?

Christmas came and went. We survived the chaos and Jacynthe did not leave me in the street. (Although I'm sure there were times when she thought about it!)

We were driving over to my friend's house, which was only one block from the hospital. We arrived there in the afternoon and my mom and Jacynthe started their food for the special dinner. My dad tried to figure out how I would have my own dinner. Nothing special for me. It would be the same thing every day until I moved out of the hospital, and even then, I'd have to wait seven more months after my admission. I ate from a J-tube in my stomach, two bottles of Ensure at every meal. My OT made it clear right from the start: no food for me or I die.

My Dad arranged something from the swing's frame of the friend's baby. I had a real Christmas with presents and the big dinner. I could only watch but that was all good because everyone was happy — me the most — to celebrate all together outside the hospital.

The following day I had a very awkward moment with Jacynthe. She needed to replace my catheter. Don't laugh because it was not funny! At least my mom wasn't doing it! I am so thankful that Jacynthe was there, because she was the only person I would ever let do that.

I stayed at the Foothills hospital: two weeks at the ICU (Intensive Care Unit), one month at Unit 12 and finally, seven months in Unit 58, for a total of nine months. I was then transferred to Ponoka for thirteen months. I was in rough shape back then. I was living day to day. I had no clue that someday I would be living on my own, writing a book and making my own Internet site.

By the way, I've done this all from scratch, not even knowing what I was doing. Not too shabby, hey?

Unit 58 was the rehabilitation unit of the Foothills hospital. Every day I needed to attend some sort of rehabilitation, mainly from the big three groups of therapies: Physiotherapy, Occupation and Speech.

I also had access to counselling because it was at Unit 58 where I attempted suicide. My situation seemed hopeless, not being able to talk and barely being able to move. I knew also my relationship with the love of my life was pretty much over.

Some people don't understand why I'm still good friends with Jass, my ex-wife. I don't blame her for our situation, and I would probably do the same thing if the roles were reversed. She's a very active person and everything was so complicated with me.

When we filed for divorce, my lawyer did not want to go through with it, saying that I can't give everything to her and be left with nothing. She was assuming that my judgment was affected by my condition. What could have been a very straightforward divorce was complicated by the perception of this lawyer.

Finally, after numerous meetings, I persisted on going ahead with the divorce. I never doubted that this was the right thing to do. Even after twelve years, I'm still glad of my decision and I am thankful that the lawyer was able to understand that this was something I needed to do. People have always tried to categorize me, only to realize that I don't fit into the regular frames.

In due time I was transferred to Ponoka. I didn't even know this place existed, let alone know where it was. All I knew was that I was going, but I had no idea what I would be doing.

Chapter 20
Ponoka (2007–2008)
Schooldays!

I 'escaped' my rehabilitation center at the Foothills hospital and was taken to the Centennial Center for Mental Health and Brain Injury in the town of Ponoka, Alberta.

It has an excellent reputation and people come from all over the world for its renowned mental health programs. Some people even say that it is the best of the best! The Centennial Center has everything under the same roof, including a pub (alcohol free), coffee shop, bank and so much more. It's amazing!

We had a schedule every week. How busy you were depended on your stamina. For me, I was very busy in the morning and usually two hours in the afternoon. I reserved the two other ones for my nap, which was much needed. I had few free time slots here and there, but not many.

My days were full of ongoing rehabilitation, non-stop for thirteen months. I took part in Physiotherapy, Occupation Therapy, Speech Therapy, Psychology, Recreation Therapy and groups like Range of Motion, Problem Solving, Games and more.

I was in a double room at first. Then I went on strike and stopped shaving in protest. The head nurse finally caved and gave me a single room to keep me happy.

There were three separate units for brain injury and the doors were always locked. Only a few people had a key, since some patients were unable to find their way back through the facility. I was one of the lucky few who had a key.

You'll meet some very interesting individuals in a rehab center!

My neighbor, who did not talk, walk or move around, slept in a cage and made the same noise over and over. To keep him quiet, the nurses would put on a DVD of Johnny Cash. The same DVD played for ten hours a day, 365 days a year and he still enjoyed it.

Poor guy, he did not have a schedule. Nobody wanted him, so the center was stuck with him. He had nowhere to go. He was there for five years, and I bet he's probably still there, all these years later.

Back to what was going to write. I left Ponoka on Friday evening (Friday) for Canmore, which was about three hours away. Canmore is the town where Jacynthe lives and where I used to live as well.

We were registered for a five-kilometer road race. Some people push their babies. Jacynthe would push me in my manual wheelchair. It had been a while since I'd been around so many people.

Good thing we were not going for gold, because the front castor vibrated like crazy when Jass gave 'er hard. Once we began to cruise, it was all good.

A very good friend pushed her cute little baby in his stroller and ran along with us. We had supporters along the way. My parents came for the week, so they were there to cheer us up. It was a wonderful experience. I would have preferred to run but now I'm pushed and that is all right.

Sunday, before going back to the center, we took the gondola to the summit of Sulfur Mountain in Banff. The gondola goes from city level all the way up into the alpine. A lazy way to go up the mountain but it was perfect for my new lifestyle. I enjoyed going up there. After all these years I'm still driven by the mountains. The only problem is, I can't go to them!

In Ponoka I was fortunate to have good therapists. At the time I thought they were mean to want me to take my shower, go to the bathroom and go to bed on my own. Now, I would like to thank them for giving me a kick in the butt! Even after all these years, I am grateful for their encouragement. I believe that because of it, I was able to work toward living on my own, and to create the ideal situation to build a better life for myself. Step by step, I began to accept the new me.

If Jass wasn't there, I would be probably still in a group home and not writing this book. I can also credit her for giving me a kick in the butt first!

In the earlier time in Ponoka, life was simply waking up in the morning, food (if we can call that pureed stuff food), programs, watching the wall and bed. The same routine day after day.

Jass was about to end that era; she drove three hours from Canmore with a brand-new computer! Yahoo! Something to do. To this day, I am totally dependent on my computer. It is part of my daily life. I used it to write this book, to make my movies, to watch TV shows, make my Internet site, to write (prediction software), to read (text to speech software), to print, and more. The list is endless!

Two times a month, Jass would drive six hours round trip in a day, just to spend time with me. We were not allowed to have guests overnight at the center. No exception was made for family, even if we were still married at the time. Jass couldn't afford a motel every time she came to visit, and because there were none in the small town of Ponoka, she would have had to drive thirty minutes out of her way to Red Deer for a decent room anyway. Thankfully, Jass was there for me, because I would have been so lonely otherwise.

Often, when she would visit, we would go on outings. One outing involved staying at a motel in Red Deer. To spice it up a bit we took a room with a hot tub. We had no problem getting in the hot tub, but it was quite another story when it came to getting back out again. In fact, being all wet and slippery, the tub was slippery too. Jass couldn't pull me out.

While Jass was crying on the bed, I was freezing, all wet in the tub. It took about fifteen minutes before we were finally successful, and I was again on dry land.

Also, to break the routine, we escaped once more to Red Deer for a movie day. After the show, I needed to visit the "can" (toilet). Done with my business, Jass was transferring me and lifting my pants, when I slipped and fell to the ground. I was not hurt but it was impossible for her to put me back in my wheelchair. I was willing to help but there wasn't much I could do.

Jass was only 5' 4" and weighed 110 pounds, but she never let her small physique stop her from taking me out. At that moment, though, she was very upset and felt useless trying to put me back up on my wheels. She asked for help from someone. I don't know who felt the most embarrassed, her or me?

During the summer, it was a challenge to find things to do outside of my four walls. It was also very boring. Jass spotted a lake on the map, not too far away. The medical people at the center warned us to avoid any uncontrolled water because of the J-tube in my stomach. Getting an infection would not be good. They said a pool would be better with all the chlorine, but still not ideal.

After shopping for a floating tube and trying it out, we realized that my J-tube was not even close to being submerged. We decided to take the risk and go to the lake. We went three times in the water and Jass's parents even joined us a few times.

Even though we are not together any more, Jass continues to help and support me. Now I will ruin the nice rhythm of this book and jump into the future for few minutes. She's my only real "family" in Alberta.

She's very busy with her two kids (not mine), and we don't see as much of each other. The situation should improve as her two kids are getting older. I feel very much loved by Jass and her family. Her mom makes me feel like I'm very important and her sister is more than a friend.

I feel that I'm still part of the family. They live far away in northern Quebec at the border of Labrador. I made a trip in 2014 and loved it so much that I wanted to go back, but bad timing got in the way. I loved it so much because I went ripping it up with a four-wheeler (side by side) almost every day.

I've never said it out loud, but writing this book made me realize how much your support means to me and I want to thank you, Jass, for not leaving me to fight this journey alone!

Now back to where we were: when I thought I had found a good plan to go back into the mountains, I seemed to experience failure after failure, but at least I had found a group home that I liked!

Chapter 21
Rijamo (2008–2013)
Home, Sweet Home!

I arrived in my new group home, determined to exercise and train in preparation for my next big climb.

The owner of the group home was awesome; he installed my contraption for doing half pull-ups from my own bed. It was basically a set of two ropes with handles at the ends mounted to a 4x4 screwed in the ceiling. With my cuff to keep a grip with my right hand, I did two sets of 100 half pull-ups three times a week.

I wanted to climb Mount Yamnuska in the front ranges of the Canadian Rockies. I started to climb again right after I came out of the hospital in 2009. Since my accident, I had learned to climb in my own unique way.

By 2011, my system was very slick, with only having my physical limitations to stop me. This made me realize when I have only my condition to limit me, I should aim to set the bar high.

I wanted to climb a new route which was 350 meters high. It was an extremely hard route, but I didn't care because I would climb the wall and not the rock. I picked that wall because it was mostly overhanging all the way.

My support team wanted to see me climb 200 meters at the Back of the Lake in Lake Louise. They figured that by the time I did that climb I would be even stronger. I even did the last leg strongest of all, covering the distance of twenty-five meters in ten minutes. I did the 200 meters without any issues and showed everyone that I could do it! My support team consisted of James Madden, Nick Rapaich, Pat Delaney and Will Gadd. They are all still involved in mountain guiding.

Fall 2011... No go! Summer 2012... No go! Fall 2012... No go! The next attempt would be my last.

Everything was ready to go except for a lack of volunteers to take me to the base of the route. We were looking for twenty-five and only had twenty. I had trained for one and half years, three time a week. The next possible attempt was in the summer 2013... Forget it! I'm out!

This was, honestly, one of the best group homes in Calgary! The owners, especially Richard Benasen, tried to run this group home like a real home. We were treated like a big family. We would have BBQs in the summer, celebrate holidays together, share big Christmas presents. I felt like I was welcome and even loved, almost like one of their kids. Richard was even my volunteer twice a week at the gym and once a week swimming. He was always willing to help and fix my things.

The location was probably also the best. Located across the street from Lake Midnapore, only one minute from a path that leads you to Fish Creek Park. Lake Midnapore is thirty acres big and Fish Creek is 13.3 kilometers.

On a warm summer day, Lake Midnapore was my go-to. It was a great escape, especially with the 4x4 wheelchair and its chair recliner. I would head there for few hours, park myself under a tree, recline the seat and listen to an audiobook.

On the cold but blue-sky days of fall I did the same. There was not a soul in the park. I would settle my chair by the water, listen to the audiobook and observe the ducks for few hours. And every time, I would think to myself: I'm living the life!

Fish Creek Park was a paradise for me. Nature in the city, only five minutes from my door. It was full of trails that I used to ride. For a guy like me, Fish Creek and Lake Midnapore created a true paradise. In the last two snow-free seasons I was able to take my 4x4 wheelchair everywhere, since it was easier to drive. When I had to move into the city, the 4x4 became useless and pointless to drive so I donated it, with my trailer, to Rocky Mountain Adaptive.

I liked to imagine myself resting peacefully in my old age in a place like this group home in Midnapore. If it were not for the closure, I would never have moved.

One morning, Richard came for a chat. Totally out of the blue, he told me that in one week from now he would have to close the home down! It was all because of a city rule that required the home to have fire walls. It would have cost $140,000 to install and would take a year to do. I could not believe it, until the caseload manager came to confirm the worst.

Everything came crashing down on me — I felt as if my life were being destroyed! I was so upset and angry that I even contacted the Mayor's office about the situation. After a bunch of emails, it was determined that even the Mayor cannot reverse a decision of the Fire Marshal. I often wonder why the Fire Marshal got involved in the first place.

Even today, I miss the place sometimes, but life continues, and we need to just go with it!

Anyway, we got shipped all over the city and I ended up moving to Saddletowne. Lucky me.

Chapter 22
Saddletowne (2013–2015)
Roll, roll away!

Thank heaven for the YMCA. Because I did not like my group home, I spent most of my free time there. I used the reclining bike for a minimum of two hours each time, two or three times a week. There was a TV on the bike, so I would watch the Outdoor Life Network which helped make the time fly by.

When I was not at the Y, I kept myself busy at the In-Definite Arts Program, doing kung fu, power chair soccer and hockey, sit-skiing or sailing.

When I was not working out, I volunteered at the climbing gym. I put the kids on the auto belay. Believe it or not, I had a high position with the climbing gym. However, while the YMCA is more focused on recreation, I was more focused on performance. Based on our different opinions, I decided to leave on my own before they fired me!

Once a week I went swimming. By myself! That's right! I was tired of my volunteer not showing up, so I asked if an employee could switch my chair while I'm standing up at the grab bar and wheel me in the pool area. It took them less than five minutes. Plus, it gave them something different to do once a week.

At the pool they put a life jacket and fins on me. Then

they put me in the water. Two lifeguards each held onto a handle of the water wheelchair. From both sides of the ramp, they lowered the chair into the water. That way they were able to put me in the water without getting wet.

Once in the water, I would float on my back and kick with the fins. My best performance was forty lengths (one kilometer) in an hour and half. Afterwards, I would always go into the hot tub, but with a life jacket. That way there was no stress and I could relax by myself.

Then I would go home, with my swimsuit dripping, even in the winter! Just kidding!

I couldn't stand but I was able to bridge. The employee would first put a plastic bag and then a towel on the cushion of my wheelchair. As I stood at the grab bar, they'd switch me into the wheelchair.

When I had no one to assist me, I learned how to bridge on my own, unloading my cushion, as I removed my swimsuit, towel and plastic bag. It took me few years, but I figured it out. This was in 2013. To this day, I swim solo, every week. Swimming is something I still — and always — will do!

Maybe you're curious as to why I don't talk about my group home? Let's just say that my ideal living situation was not to reside in an institute. I was renting a small room and I could not even do what I wanted with my space. I could not store something outside my room which was totally new for me. I needed to put my 4X4 wheelchair at the YMCA or sell it. It was in the basement of the YMCA for a year and a half and I took it out only twice because I had nowhere to ride it.

Then one very strange day, everything seemed to go downhill.

First off, I take many pills. Because of this, I developed a lactose and gluten intolerance due to high acidity in my stomach. I had never heard of such a thing, and neither had any of my doctors. So, I was taking a pill to cure my lactose and gluten problem when I reacted to the pill in question and was admitted to the Emergency. They did a bunch of tests and they were unable to find the problem. Then I began experiencing vertigo, but they proceeded to kick me out of the ER anyway.

Basically, I was experiencing a high. I was drugged! A group took me with force to the waiting room, where I woke up a few hours later covered in my own pee. They had called the police and I was to be arrested! Fortunately, they had no way to carry me in my heavy wheelchair. Instead, they called a handi-taxi to take me home. They must have figured I was a very weak criminal and let me go. The story does not end there but I will stop whining!

After that event, almost everybody thought I was a liar including my caseload manager. From then on, our relationship became complicated.

The owner of the group home evicted me a few months later because I was breaking too many rules and had blown off too many curfews. I found and made all the arrangements myself for what would be my next place. I did not have any help at all from Alberta Health Services.

My first group home cared in a way that was completely different from this one. My next move would prove to be an epic one!

Chapter 23
Thank you! (sarcastic)

I was in downtown Calgary. I was going to visit an apartment for rent and was given the impression that it was a deluxe apartment. I imagined it was wide open and well lit. That the convenience store was in the lobby, not outside.

It was a rental to share with a dude I had never met. We both wanted to move away from our group home as soon as possible. Our plan was to rent a one-bedroom apartment. One person would stay in the living room. Because we were both in wheelchairs, we would put a band of cardboard around the place to protect the walls from dings. We would even take the doors off if we needed to get around.

Right from the beginning, everything went wrong — the apartment had already been rented, and my potential roommate didn't even bother to show up. Good thing it didn't work out. The building, which I thought was built in 2000, was actually built in the 70s. Everything was so tight, I don't think we could have even fitted through the front door! I didn't see the bathroom, but I bet we wouldn't have fitted in there either.

It was a crazy idea by two desperate men who needed to move out ASAP. My only option was Calgary Housing, but I could be on the waiting list for another year! My eviction date was overdue by a month and a half and I needed to get out.

Since the other guy didn't show up (I would later learn that there was a problem with the handi-bus), I decided to go exploring. That idea was short-lived. It was the middle of winter and about five centimeters of snow had fallen the day before. The sidewalks were still a mess, which meant that my exploration consisted of only one block in every direction.

Back home, I searched and searched on the Internet for a better arrangement. I came across, an ad about a brand-new build building right downtown (www.1010center.ca). There were some units available, even a few to accommodate a wheelchair. A building for low income, single, no alcohol allowed and no visitors past midnight (better than eight p.m. in the group home).

I imagined escaping, finally, to a place for a better lifestyle. As an added note, I promised not to get my hopes up. I'm very proud of the next chapter in my life and that is why I want to share it with you.

The same evening, I completed all the forms requested and sent it off. The following day, they asked me to attend a meeting. I saw the apartment for the first time. It seemed a little crowded with all the furniture. I would need to leave behind my Meywalker (www.meyland-smith.dk/en/).

Then, they checked my references and I was ready to move in two weeks later. At first, I did not see the potential. After a month, I realized all the modifications I would need to do in order to accommodate my special needs.

I organized everything myself including the moving, the special equipment, Home Care, shopping and all my address changes. The group home asked me if I needed help, of course, but it was too late. With only one week until my departure, everything was already done!

I was about to relive the bachelor lifestyle... with a few modifications.

Chapter 24
Downtown Calgary (2015–2017)
With Style!

At this time, I'd taken kung fu lessons for five years and achieved a level V sash. My kung fu private session had just ended, and I was waiting twenty-five meters from the city bus stop. I was always told to wait there and wave at the driver when he comes by. The bus stop is on a sidewalk with no access at all for my wheelchair.

The bus arrived and slowed down to contour me in the street. The driver saw me waving. He waved back but did not stop. I'm thinking in my head #@$%$, he is stupid or what? The next bus was in thirty minutes and I had my Art class at one p.m. I refused to have my day all wrecked, since I found out that Jacynthe, my ex-wife, delivered her second child Zoe that morning.

After my Art class I had an appointment at the wheelchair shop. Most would probably think I should have complained. I say it just wasn't worth it! At best I might have gotten an apology, or some recognition. But it was not worth the time and effort. Anyway, I decided to go to Chinook Station by wheelchair and make it on time for my next bus.

Some people fear the unknown, but not me! I used the opportunity to find a challenge. That was the only thing giving me at least 5% of the overall adrenaline I was used too. So, for me it was not a big deal. I've lived the adventure can take what life throws at me. I'm better taking the bus.

Since I'd moved, I refused to take the handicap bus during the snow-free months. I lived downtown and had access to a wide selection of buses and trains. Before I was taking the Transit for short distance only. Being here gave me the chance to go all over the place.

I was able to go shopping at IKEA, and travel to my In-Definite Art and kung fu programs, to Mount Royal University, Foothills hospital, Vivo (my power hockey) and many more places. When the snow was on the ground, I was stuck with the handicap bus.

Taking Transit was giving me another 2.5% of adrenaline. A guy takes as much as he can! The Transit bus was always on time, the handicap bus was sometimes late or early, but rarely right on the money!

I'm finally free! After all these years (nine years), I can say that nobody is "spying" or keeping tabs on my whereabouts.

One night, I went to see Cirque du Soleil with my handicapped friends (one is in a power wheelchair and the other one walks with a cane). We walked from my apartment because it was so close.

On the way I took the lead and I got to a point where I needed to cross the road. There were no marks on the sidewalk where the ramp was. I took a good look around and went where I thought the ramp would be (remember, I see only in 2D). It turned out that there was no ramp and because I was going so slowly, I didn't clear the sidewalk. The back of my chair was still on the sidewalk and the front was stuck on the street. I had the reflexes to put my good leg on the street and was able to lift my chair and myself back onto the sidewalk.

Cirque du Soleil was amazing! My friend in a wheelchair asked us what we were the most impressed with. For me, it was the guys jumping on the big trampoline. For him, even after seeing all those amazing athletes, he said that what impressed him the most, was me lifting my wheelchair with only one leg! For the first time I realized that I was maybe one of a kind.

I loved my new apartment! It was small but I liked it that way. Less space to spread out and be out of control. Also, the messes were smaller but still frequent, as I was still adjusting my lifestyle.

For example (of course by accident), I used to put frozen blueberries in my cereal. One morning I dropped the contents of the complete bag of blueberries on the floor. By the time I put the blueberries in a pile under the counter, left for my caregiver to pick it up (I'm not able to use a dustpan), the blueberries were taut and juicy. The floor of the kitchen was all stained purple. Almost red, it looked like somebody was murdered in the kitchen and somebody cleaned the blood but not all. Since that day, I've eaten no more blueberries for breakfast. That was by far my biggest mess, but smaller ones are quite frequent. I had an awesome caregiver that was quite understanding of the limits of a handicapped person living on his own.

I did some modifications for the apartment to be more wheelchair friendly. First, I got someone to take off the bathroom door and put it behind the fridge. Then I got a shower curtain to replace the door. I paid all together $8 for the curtain and pole. I also needed to protect the walls from my wheelchair, so I got a box of laminate floor for $16. One box is all I needed. It did the job and it looked good.

I completely changed the bedroom and I replaced my twenty-six-inch computer screen for a forty-inch. I was able to see what was on the screen, which was a big benefit to finishing this book. I could honestly say that I loved my apartment with all the modifications. Thank you, Jamie, for helping me out. Without you my quality of life would have been terrible.

I received reinforcements twice a week by my caregiver. One of those two days, she did my laundry. During that time, she helped me with my shower transfers, washing my back and hair. She also washed my dishes and kept the place neat.

Food could be a bit tricky or very simple, depending on how you see it! I used microwave technology a lot... and I mean a lot! I was getting to be a professional chef with the microwave. I don't use the stove because I don't want to burn my building down. To make things easy, I use only frozen meals. The first couple of weeks I was putting the meals in the microwave straight from the freezer. That was super gross!

I learned to leave the meal on the counter in the morning. In the evening, I just needed to put it in the microwave a fraction of the time. Now everything is warm (not burned or still frozen) and it tasted good. I eat better than when I was in the group homes. Sometimes I used the toaster oven to warm meals.

Getting groceries was another big deal. Especially during the winter when I couldn't get around as much. Sometimes, I had a hard time getting from the front door to the handicap bus because of the snow. In that case, there is no question: I had to ask for help. I was always able to find someone from my many friends on Facebook. It was easy! Just a small post and I'd get an answer right away.

Every week for two years I dedicated one day for grocery shopping. (Preferably in the afternoons, because I am not a morning person. I usually don't start to get my butt into gear until around noon.)

I took the C-train to the Westbrook Walmart. I picked that store because the C-train station is underground. Snowfall, cold — I didn't care because I'm protected from the elements.

I still use the same technique today, I just don't go every week.

I would bring a heavy-duty bag and leave it resting on my footplate with one strap of the bag through my seat belt. I picked what I needed and put it in the bag. Usually, I'd have less than eight items and go to the quick checkout.

I liked Walmart, mostly for their cashier system. There are usually about six cashiers, and since it takes me some time to go through, at least there's not somebody impatient waiting in line behind me. The cashier would help me unload and reload the bag on my wheelchair on the back handles.

Then I would go back to the C-train station and go home to unload. I was extra careful on the C-train and the elevator to not squish my groceries. Sometimes I felt like I needed a sign saying, "Careful, overloaded!"

Now, I shop online for dry foods, cleaning supplies, hygiene stuff, anything that is non-perishable. For any order of $50 or over, the delivery is free at Walmart. Finally, I don't have to pay extra for small quantities. This has helped me so much. My life has become too busy to reserve one day just for grocery shopping!

My apartment was right downtown by the famous Calgary Tower! The Stampede was only five minutes away. 17th avenue (famous for the NHL Flames Red Mile) was close by. Stephen Avenue was also near; filled with musicians and festivals going on almost every week during the summer.

I felt that I could at last relax and enjoy the city. Not having to worry about my living arrangements was a huge relief. I really, really loved my place and the lifestyle it gave me. I loved that it was a central location. I was a city boy and felt that I would never leave this place. Maybe, when I'm very old and can't get around on my own — then I might have to consider my options!

Chapter 25
The New Remy by Chic Scott

The stroke that Remy Bernier suffered on October 18, 2006 left him severely disabled. His right arm and right leg are almost completely paralyzed. He is almost deaf in his right ear. His vocal cords are also half paralyzed making his speech very difficult to understand. And his vision is severely compromised in many ways. It is a hard burden to bear.

But Remy is a fighter and always has been. As one of his friends, Tom Parks, says, "It was not in Remy's personality to give up before the stroke, so he was not about to give up after the stroke. He is almost more fearless now."

Remy has remade his life: he 'skis', he plays power hockey, he has created his own website and several videos, he has 'climbed' vertical cliffs and makes beautiful artworks.

According to another friend, Jonathan Silvernagle, "Remy is still very driven, very ambitious. He doesn't let his stroke hold him back."

Jean Francois Monette, Remy's old friend from his high school days, says, "I always thought that Remy was the best guy to live that struggle. He is the type of guy who can go through any struggle and keep his head high."

Despite his disabilities Remy is still the same person inside heart and mind and his motivation is incredible, impressing all his friends. Jamie Everett, a volunteer instructor with the Canadian Association of Disabled Skiers who helped Remy with the sit ski program for about four years at Canada Olympic Park, says that Remy had some pretty bad crashes early in his career and even broke a sled but did not give up. In Jamie's opinion, "Remy already knows skiing and accepts that he might crash. He is already very risk-tolerant. Remy pushes through adversity more than many people with disabilities, likely because of his climbing background."

Amazingly, Remy had a dream of ascending the 350-meter-high cliff of Yamnuska by jumaring the rope with mechanical ascenders. It was an audacious idea and he almost succeeded. First, he practiced on several smaller cliffs. With the help of friends from Rocky Mountain Adaptive and from the climbing community, he was wheeled to the base of the cliffs at Grassi Lakes. Here he jumared to the top of the wall at a route called Holey S#@$ which is completely overhanging.

On another occasion with the help of many friends he jumared to the top of a twenty-five-meter cliff near Lake Louise. It must have been very scary, hanging there in space but Remy did it. There was, however, always a top rope on Remy so he could be lowered down at any time if there were problems.

Unfortunately, Remy's dream of 'climbing' Yamnuska never was fulfilled because he could not pull together a big enough team of volunteers to get him to the base of the cliff.

Alison Blanchard, a good friend of Remy who works with disabled adults thinks that people with disabilities have a right to make choices and to perhaps even fail. "When people take care of you and feed you and make decisions for you, you lose your sense of self. Remy never lost that."

One of Remy's biggest frustrations is that people have great difficulty in understanding him when he speaks. According to Jonathan, "People immediately give up when they meet Remy. Because they can't understand him, they think he is slow or brain damaged. But he is not, he is all there."

The great support in Remy's life has been Jass. Dealing with Remy's stroke has been very difficult for her, but she cares very deeply for Remy, is pragmatic and has given Remy incredible support. Remy was young when his stroke happened, and all his friends were young. Life goes on for everyone and his young friends have gone their separate ways, something that has been hard for Remy to watch. But Jass is still there for him.

According to his friends Remy is very sociable and is always the first to introduce himself and engage when he meets new people. People gravitate towards him because of his energy. But Remy can be difficult too. He can be demanding, can blow up and be angry. According to one friend, "He has his fiery Quebecois side." In fact, sometimes he undermines his own projects — those who are trying to help him can get fed up with him.

And he has a strong sense of justice and the courage to stand up for what he thinks is right. When he had his difficulties at the group home RIJAMO he held his ground. According to Remy, "When two strong heads are going 'head to head', one needs to get out and I wasn't going anywhere! If I wasn't standing so much for myself, they wouldn't quit. I believe in justice and human rights, when those rights are against the handicapped, I won't simply shut up."

Many people admire the strength that Remy has shown through adversity. Alison Blanchard says, "I take inspiration from Remy, I am in awe of him. It would have been so easy for him to stay in the group home and just let people take care of him. But he fought and said, 'I'm not going to take this.'"

Tom Wolfe who suffered a serious accident while working as a guide and is going through a long healing process says, "Remy's experience has been a real example after my accident. To see his courage and determination is very inspirational."

According to Jamie, Remy wants to be as independent as he can. Jamie has made adaptations to Remy's apartment at the 1010 Center in downtown Calgary which have helped him to live an independent life. One of his big contributions was the single-handed toilet paper dispenser. Having only one good hand makes life very difficult at times and this device was very helpful.

Remy loves music, some of his favorites being the Black Keys, Red Hot Chili Peppers, Yes and Mumford and sons. He is a big fan of the Montreal Alouettes and the Canadiens. Together with Tom and Jonathan he goes to concerts, football games, movies and the Cirque de Soleil.

Remy also has an artistic side through which he can express his passion for climbing and still be connected to the mountains. Through his videos Remy can reach out to the community and promote the opportunities that disabled people have. He wants to inspire disabled people and encourage them to be active and engaged.

According to Alison, "Remy puts no blocks in his way so potentially he could do anything he set his mind to." She feels that it's all in your attitude and your future is what you make of it.

"I don't think Remy's mind ever stops," says Tom Parks. "When he gets onto something he is totally committed."

According to Jonathan "Remy is proud of himself and what he has accomplished. Depression is not in his vocabulary. Remy complains sometimes but it is never about the challenges."

PART 3:
NO REST FOR THE WICKED

Chapter 26
Deception after Deception!

I started as a movie maker just after my two years in hospital. I wanted to express myself because I couldn't and decided that multimedia would be my best option.

I had everything to learn — from planning to realization. I picked up software for $30 and learned to use it as I went.

In the meantime, Wade from the popular "Night of Lies" (a not so serious slideshow competition held in Canmore, mostly about climbing) heard about my movie making. He approached me to be part of the 2009 edition. I needed to do a good job — there would be 300 spectators viewing my work. I took my task seriously... and I delivered.

From my desk in the group home, armed with my modest software program, I began to work on my first movie/slideshow. I was extremely proud about the outcome. There was not a dry eye in the audience, and I won by a large margin!

Even today, many years after the fact, I think about this very true moment of my extraordinary past life, and I will always be very proud of the outcome. YouTube: *Remy's Life* — short

The following year, I was back to NOL. Even with what little experience I had, I still felt that I did amazing work with my computer. This time I got second place and the only standing ovation.

This made me very confident that I would be screened at the Banff Festival, but unfortunately, my movie was far from their high standards. There is a huge degree of difference between the NOL and the Banff Festival, and I had simply no idea of what it would take to make it further.

This was my first deception. 2011 was the year. YouTube: Remy's war

I will go back at the NOL in 2012 but I did a mediocre job with similar outcome.

In 2013, I started work on *Remy Goes Four-by-Fouring*. This was the first project I committed to doing on my own. Next came *Remy's Adventures* with Shaw Calgary. I started a new era with the latter, as the man behind the scenes, as well as the one in front of the camera taking part in the adventures.

In 2016, Shaw Calgary and I went all out in the test piece *Adapt*. No question — I felt that this would be the one to screen at the Banff Festival, but again, it did not make the cut. It was very discouraging. I realized then that maybe I was not at the extremely high level of the Banff Festival

After that, my movie *Adapt* did not even make the cut at disability festivals.

At the Focus on Ability Short Film Festival, I was 100 percent sure my *Remy's Adventures* sledge hockey and swimming piece would win first prize — but I never received a phone call. *Remy's Adventures — swimming*" also failed at the Calgary International Film Festival.

Even if I were to create better films in the future, I probably won't fare well at the disability festivals. This is because I make action-based films, while the films that have a sentimental touch usually win.

On the other hand, there is still a lot of emotion in my movies, but far less than the one taking the grand prize. Perhaps I will do better in regular festivals, but the competition is so serious, and the number of submissions is so high that my chances are almost impossible. I will continue to make excellent movies, but I don't think they will ever make it on-screen.

So, during that time, I had spent close to $300 and with absolutely nothing in return. I could never make a better movie than *Adapt*. It seemed that my only chance of success was to go back to when I was creating my movie alone, but I would need way more than my $30 software.

I learned a lot from that previous year, and I put all the odds on my side. I will still pursue this path but, let us say, that I'm taking it way less seriously and I will never again make assumption without facts. It's way, way, too depressing to do so.

UPDATE:

Everybody seems to think I'm making movies to be famous. This perception of me is completely incorrect and is not the case at all!

When I came out of the hospital, I was obsessed with watching adventure films. It became a strong form of therapy, giving me the drive needed to write a book and finish it one day. Having this specific goal has kept me in check all these years.

That said; I literally live for my movies. I'm obsessed in the most extreme way. I have all the Reel Rock DVDs and have watched them more times than I can remember. My collection also includes some ski movies and a whole collection of other climbing movies. I can't help it, I'm watching now, the best TV show ever made, *Ultimate Alaskan Survivor* season II and III for the fourth time.

My favorites include Reel Rock 9, 10 and 11, as well as the ski movie, *Attack of La Nina*.

I listen to audiobooks related to climbing or the same spirit, every day, usually in transit on my way to an appointment or program.

My ultimate goal is to have my movie on screen at a festival. This is my biggest dream and I couldn't care less about being famous. If it happens one day, great! Until then I will continue to get more out of each experience.

For instance, I've already applied five times to the Vancouver International Mountain Film Festival, and I have no plans to stop applying. Year after year, my movies are getting better, and I really do believe that I'm now on the verge of making it! In my opinion, I feel I could cross that line at any time now, and I will keep making movies until I make it on screen.

Chapter 27
My City

I love my city. I love the public transportation. It offers me all the tools to be as independent as I am. Good thing I'm not in Montreal with all the snow and lack of accessibility. I consider myself quite lucky, but my city is far from perfect.

I once tried to cross the C-train tracks and the lines that mark the slope were absent. With my vision problem, I could not see where the slope was, so I guessed. Turns out, only one wheel was on the slope and the other was on the curb. When the light turned green, my chair flipped, and I landed across the train track, on the ground, strapped to my 300-pound wheelchair. Two strong guys helped me by putting me back on my two wheels. Not even two minutes later, a train was passing by. That was a super close one, I almost did not have a chance to finish this book.

I realized how difficult it could be to plan a trip when I was dropped off at a stop and there was no physical way to get on the street, other than to go off-road, onto the grass and then jump the curb. In these instances, I am grateful for my adventurous nature!

Sometimes, there were obstacles. At the Indefinite Arts location, there was a bench blocking the path to get onto the bus. During the snow-free months, I had managed by driving my motorized wheelchair on the grass. But in the winter, I was forced to take the handicap bus. I preferred the regular bus, as it dropped me off very close to my place. Instead, I had to take the handicap bus, which gets me home much later. This situation was really affecting me.

The city had been made aware of these issues, but it took six months for the city to finally move the park bench. After my first notice, the city told me that the bench provider had been notified. They just needed to get two guys and move it one foot forward.

After my second notice and a threat to block the circulation of the bus route by waiting in the street, the city finally moved the bench forward!

Another time, there was a car constantly parking at the exit of the Chinook Mall pedestrian overpass. I always ended up making a detour to get where I needed to go.

Tired of seeing this problem, I contacted the city, but they told me that it was not their responsibility. I then contacted the land manager of the car park, and he told me that it would take some time, but he would get on it.

To me, the solution was simple. All they needed to do was write with paint on the asphalt: No Parking! I was tempted, every time to scratch the faulty car, but I'm way more civilized than that. They finally took care of the issue after eight months.

Sometimes I wonder if people even consider their actions — it can be so frustrating!

Chapter 28
Magic Bus!

In 2017, after a February snowstorm, I was forced to take the Access bus to the Eau Claire YMCA. I thought I would show some responsibility. I was taking this bus to this address for the first time and I was not familiar with this exit. The driver came to pick me up, but instead of taking the slope, he took the curb.

I followed him but in two seconds, I had flipped my heavy wheelchair into a snowbank. I ended up flat on the ground of the parking lot. Because of the snow build-up from the storm, we could not see the right way. I was totally fine, but the driver was freaking out! It's a good thing that this had happened to me and not somebody else. If it had been any other client, I truly believe that it would have been a disaster!

I try to go somewhere almost every day. I spend as little time home as possible. Not working, the days are still very long, and I would go insane if I wasn't able to go out.

In the summer of 2016, my electric wheelchair broke down and I was confined to my apartment for a what seemed like a very long week! To keep myself busy, I worked on my book. The only thing that chased away the sound of silence was the radio. I had Internet TV but only one channel.

It is very important to me to go places, even in the winter. I would love to live in Canmore for the proximity of the mountains, but Calgary has the public transportation I need. I can get anywhere in the city with Access Calgary (handicap bus). During the winter weeks I average about seventeen trips per week.

When I lived downtown, I traveled only with Access Calgary during the winter, when it rained, or for special occasions. And when I took Calgary Transit, all the routes I needed to get around the city were accessible nearby my place. This was a big advantage to living downtown! I was getting picked up in the back alley instead of the slushy street. Before that, I would have to wait at least half an hour for my wheels to dry, otherwise the floor of my apartment was always a big mess when the snow was on the street.

The percentage of nightmare trips I experienced was low, but it takes only one experience to remember it for a long, long time.

I remember my first "no-show." I was waiting for the bus on time, and the driver simply forgot to pick me up.

The second and third time, he went to the wrong place. The fourth and fifth time, the driver was there, I was there, but he never asked if I need a ride! I thought it would be obvious with my wheelchair!

The last time it happened to me, I waited four hours before I was finally picked up and able to get back home. I had skipped dinner and was almost ready to faint by the time I had food. I've been dropped off at the wrong place. And with my luck being what it was, it was pouring rain and I didn't have the proper gear with me. I had to do the one-kilometer journey in the heavy rain in order to catch my return bus!

I was soaked, but I learned something very important

that day: come prepared for any eventualities. Now I carry all the time, in my backpack, a poncho, gloves and hat. That trick had saved me dozens of times.

The system is great but not perfect. Transportation is a big thing for us in electric wheelchairs. If we are away from home, we need transportation to bring us back to point A. I speak only from my experience, but I'm sure other clients in the same situation feel the same way.

Fully equipped, I'm always ready for any other unexpected adventures. And I can deal with every situation head on. For every problem there is always a solution. It's always possible to see a bright side, even in the worst-case scenario!

Update for 2017:

I like to point out, Access Calgary has finally got their s@#$ together! At the beginning (2017) I hated the system, but since I'm on automatic scheduling, I love it. They are always on time, and because I'm automated scheduling, I have way less waiting to do. Example: The waiting period is nine forty-five for a ten oh five drop-off. Before, if I requested a drop off at ten oh five, I would wait at nine twenty and get to kung fu before the door opened. I don't believe that the system can fail any more.

Chapter 29
Advantages to Being Single-handed!

Believe it or not, there are advantages to having only one good hand (although, I think there are way more disadvantages). For example, my caregiver cleans my dishes. I hate cleaning dishes anyway, so it works out for me!

I can't perform any of the "fun" stuff around my apartment like mopping or sweeping. If I drop something on the floor and it breaks, it's hard for me to bend over and catch all the pieces with the broom. I end up having to sweep them under the counter instead, since I'm not able to use a dustpan with only one hand. My caregiver usually picks it up later for me.

If I drop liquid, it's almost the end of the world! My wheels are always in the way. By the time I get the mop, the kitchen and bathroom floors are all marked with my wheels. If the mop doesn't contain all the fluid, then I have a serious problem, since I'm not able to squeeze the water out the mop. Sometimes I just use lots of towels or cloths to sop up the spill.

That is why I use a cafeteria tray when I eat. If I spill my drink, at least it is contained within the tray. That trick (#19 of the Tricks Living In Community at nevergiveup.online) has saved me more than once and it's less effort to clean. I have a trick for almost any everyday situation.

Doing the laundry is difficult for me as well. Thank God for my wonderful caregiver who does this task once a week. I attempted it once to do it and I'm glad I don't need to do it again.

I would need a trailer on my wheelchair to carry the laundry basket to the machine which is a dozen doors down the hallway. When I get there, my wheelchair is always in the way of the machine's door. I'd need to move my wheelchair a couple of inches, open the door and keep doing this until the door is fully open.

And the best part: putting money in the machine. I'm not good with precision tasks. I have to focus, taking care not to drop the money between the washing and drying machine.

Then I have to do everything again with the dryer and make back my way to my apartment with my clothes. Finally, I have to put all my clothes into a pile in my room, since I'm unable to fold and put away my clothes. So sure, I have a wrinkle or two, but it's less work than if I tried to put it away myself!

My caregiver puts out the garbage. Another task that looks easy but almost impossible for a guy like me. I made a tool from a clothes hanger to keep the door open of the chute. I'm telling you, it's impossible without the tool. Same thing with mailbox. Every time, I need to ask assistance to put my mail in the mailbox. Cleaning up the bathroom is also a task of my caregiver. I could maybe clean the toilet but definitely not the bath, counter, sink and mirror.

So, in a nutshell, I'm exempt of all household duties for life! Not a bad deal at all! If I don't make a big mess, my caregiver will clean up after me. You see, there is always a bright side to everything, even the worst situation. I try always to do things and forget about my disabilities. That is who I am, I see myself with abilities!

Chapter 30
I'm not a Baby just Because I'm Stuck in a Wheelchair!

Some people might think I'm reckless. I'm really not! I understand the consequences of my actions. Believe me when I say: I don't want to run into problems. People judge me according to what they think people in a wheelchair can do. All that matters is that I know what I can do!

I refuse to be baby-sat and won't be limited to a controlled environment. I don't want to be treated any differently than anyone else, but my wheelchair is like a big warning sign that says: "Handle with Care, I'm Handicapped."

That is one reason why I like kung fu so much; I participate in a class with the able-bodied.

Let me reiterate: I know that I will 100-percent succeed in life. I'm quite mobile, and I can go rather far with my wheelchair. I'm not scared of the things life throws at me; this includes anything to do with water and heights.

A couple of years ago, at a summer camp, I went rafting. I told the instructor to throw me in the water with no warning. He had never seen somebody in a wheelchair who willingly wanted to get wet.

At the same camp, I was on a high rope course. I was stuck in between two stations. The instructor came to help me, but I poked her until she fell and screamed. I was laughing because I was not scared at all to be at ten meters off the ground. I was used to being in the same equipment, on a cliff, at 500 meters! Seeing all kinds of weather in my life and knowing how bad it could be, I take it all in my stride — perfect or not. I just make sure to dress well with innovative clothing. Even on a slightly cold day, I wear insulated pants with "Primaloft."

If I get stuck, there are always people ready to help. One day, I went out during an extreme blizzard; it was snowing so hard that my glasses were always covered with snow. I could barely see where I was going but, somehow, I made it back home. It just took me three times longer. When I finally got back home, I was practically a snowman on wheels. In this type of situation, some people might be hopeless and scared. Me? I love it!

My stroke was in my cerebellum, so my brain is still intact — it was the rest of my body that was affected. I'm a big thinker. If there's a problem, I always try to find a solution. I'm not afraid to ask people or friends to help me when I need a hand.

Everything else, I figure out how to do on my own. Especially with my new apartment. I'm so organized, that people are surprised with everything I can do. I'll admit, if I didn't have Internet, I could not do anything near to what I'm capable of. If I need to go somewhere, I look up the trip on the Internet, print the details, and go for it on my own using the regular bus system. Without the Internet and a printer, I would be limited to travelling on the handicap bus. That would be so boring.

I've listened to close to 100 books while waiting for either bus. Sometimes, I play games on my tablet when I'm waiting. Equipped right, I can wait a long time. Not equipped, I'm very impatient and get bored very quickly. I constantly need to have my mind occupied.

I could be as independent as possible. It does not seem to matter, as some people categorize me as very handicapped. They feel sorry for me and try to do everything for me. I get into serious arguments about my independence, and rage on the inside about the discrimination that I face.

In the summer 2016, I went rafting with camp Horizon. I had it in my mind, I was going to paddle. The three seasons prior that is what I had done, and I had just had a practice run a few weeks before on the same river while filming *Adapt*.

I'm not sure what had changed, but instead of being a part of the action, the team made me to sit in the boat and expected me to be totally passive. I was not impressed. I'm not sure what had changed, but it just goes to show that some people can't look past my handicap and see what I'm capable of!

One thing that irritates me is when people think they need to stay with me waiting for the handicap bus. I listen to audio books, so I'm equipped to wait for a long time even if the bus is late. If someone is waiting with me, I can't listen to my book. And I'm way too polite to do that while they are there. They don't realize that they are not needed at all and they can leave me. I know they have only good intentions, and I won't get mad, but I would like people to realize that I'm fine alone! I wish people could understand this, as I'm too uncomfortable to tell them myself.

Or when I need information for something as simple as the bus, and the person asks me, "Where is your care worker?" My answer is "I never had one." Sometimes they try to ignore me because they think it is not possible that I have no caregiver. Then, what should have been an easy request turns out to be complex, and by then, the bus is gone!

Chapter 32
I like to be Alone… Sometimes.

For the first time in ten years, I got stuck. Literally. I had a new electrical wheelchair and the battery ran for a very long time. I checked the service manual before my departure. According to the book, when the light is yellow, I should have had a battery life of forty-nine percent.

Next time, I will make sure to read the book more carefully. What it actually said was that yellow means an average of twenty-five to forty-nine percent. I had originally calculated twenty-four kilometers and made my way to the junction of Sarcee Trail and 16th Avenue. I turned to head back, still a long way from the Calgary Tower, where I had started my journey. My battery was still in the green. Another few kilometers, I was in the yellow. Then red. My wheelchair died underneath the 14th Street Bridge.

I called my good friend Jamie to see if he could rescue me. Luckily, he was free and lived very close to where I was stuck. Within a few minutes, he reached me and pushed me to the closest C-train station, which was Sunalta. From there, it was an easy commute to downtown. At the Center Street station, Jamie pushed me the three blocks to my apartment. Total time for the rescue mission was forty-five minutes. It would have been a nightmare if I hadn't been close to a C-train station.

I had been so impressed by the performance of my wheelchair, that I wanted to show to my friends how far I could go. I thought that this journey would be a big boost for my self-esteem, but instead, it turned out to be an embarrassing situation.

I always loved going on long strolls. Usually, more than two hours. When I was at the RIJAMO group home, I would go strolling in Fish Creek two or three afternoons a week. There were enough paved trails to drain my battery, but I was wise to never let that happen again.

The last two years as a resident, I'd head out with my 4x4 wheelchair. At that time, I had access to many back-country roads and trails. In those two years, I never had to be rescued!

When the RIJAMO group was shut down, I had to put my favorite hobby of exploring the trails on hold for two summers. This was not a good time in my life. Saddletowne was a new development, with very little access to trails and parks. I thought to myself, "What I am supposed to do if my favorite hobby is taken away from me?" The answer was the YMCA, where I passed my time working out and keeping busy in the air-conditioned facility.

Eventually, I was evicted from that rural-urban prison. I wanted to go back to RIJAMO after it reopened but my room was taken. I ended up living downtown where I had the freedom to explore again, where the Bow river had paved trails on its north and south banks. I was able to roam again for hours and could feel the freedom return! I was truly loving life again.

One of my other favorite hobbies was to listen audiobooks. I could recline in both of my wheelchairs and listen to a book for hours. I used to park at Lake Midnapore (when I was at RIJAMO) and when I lived downtown, I would go a little further to the Bow river to be by water. There was also the reservoir with a fountain at Olympic Plaza (popular green area in downtown Calgary) but it was a bit too artificial for my nature-loving ways.

When I wasn't seeking the sound of nature, I would go to Olympic Plaza or the balcony of my building.

Sometimes, when I feel lazy, I listen in my apartment while reclining in the seat of my electric wheelchair. Or I'd take the C-train on rainy days and wintery weeks, where I was always moving without the worry of driving. I'd look out the window for a couple of hours. Down the line a couple of times back and forth. Something to do...

Another way I killed time was at the TD Mall downtown. On the fourth floor is the Devonian Gardens, a massive area of green space located inside the TD Square retail mall. It's been around since 1977. It's a downtown retreat where Calgarians can go to get away from the hustle and bustle. It's where I would go to play "Angry birds" or watch a movie on my iPad. Still today, I find that destination is the best way to pass time in the winter months or on a rainy day.

Back at home, I liked to play Mario Kart on my WII video game. (And even after eight years of playing, I'm still not very good). I played the four original worlds for a while. Recently, I unlocked a fifth world. I tried to find routes where there is no way to fall off. Unfortunately, my options were limited, as I seemed to fall off all the time otherwise. It could be quite frustrating.

Bottom line, staying at home and doing nothing was

(and is) not an option for me, as I would go absolutely stir crazy!

So, these are my plans if I have a day off. Some of you might be jealous. I say that I would prefer your busy life, but I think I'm doing the best I can with my free time. I spend most of my day alone, and I'm not doing anything to fight that. I feel like I'm living in my own parallel dimension — on one side, people continue their day to day lives, while I feel like the clock has stopped. I fear that I'm wasting precious time. I try to fill in every moment I have doing as much as I can!

I consider myself a very active handicapped person. Quite possibly the *most* active. If you're able to take the time to relax and feel at ease with just sitting and taking in the world, I tip my hat to you. I don't know how you do it, but you have my admiration.

Chapter 33
I'm Hooked!

Everywhere I go, I have my iPhone on my belt. It is attached to a carabiner, in my belt loop with a homemade leash (trick #39). Super easy to access, I never miss a phone call because my phone is on auto-answer and will reroute to the speaker. My earbuds are easy to access in a little pocket on the outside of my wheelchair. I can put on the unit, ready to listen in a matter of seconds. When my bus arrives, I just need to disconnect the earbuds.

I also use my iPhone to tell the time, and when I'm out and waiting, I can listen to my book.

Before, I was using the library online of Calgary Library. I used the service for eight years. It's great but you have only access to publish book in audiobook media and you need to wait your turn if the book is taken.

I really thought that was the only way to go until I discovered Bookshare. Bookshare is strictly reserved for print disabled. Since I discovered Bookshare, new, more interesting books were finally offered to me. Bookshare uses a computer voice to read out any kind of books, including non-audiobooks. There is no waiting period and once it is downloaded, you can keep it forever. You're supposed to delete them when you're are done but, in my case, I listen to the same eleven books in a loop over and over and I never get bored.

I was already a fan of Aron Ralston with the audiobook version of *Between a Rock and a Hard Place*. Since listening to the new edition of his book with Bookshare, I'm now the ultimate fan! If you thought the audiobook version was excellent, the new edition is the bomb.

This kind of reading is right up my alley! I love it. It's so good, that it's made number one in my list of best books ever made. I tried to create a ranking system for my reading, but every time I started a book, I was going to make it number one. I decided to stop while I was ahead and present the top ten of what I consider to be the crème de la crème! (Along with a special mention, rounding out the list to eleven.)

- *Between a Rock and a Hard Place* - Aron Ralston
- ***No Shortcuts to the Top: Climbing the World's 14 Highest Peaks*** - Ed Viesturs and David Roberts
- *Alone on the Wall* - Alex Honnold and David Roberts
- *The Push: A Climber's Journey of Endurance, Risk, and Going Beyond Limits* - Tommy Caldwell
- *The Calling: A Life Rocked by Mountains* - Barry Blanchard
- *Born to Run: A Hidden Tribe, Superathletes, and the Greatest Race the World Has Never Seen* - Christopher McDougall
- *Into the Wild* - Jon Krakauer
- *Touch the Top of the World: A Blind Man's Journey to Climb Farther Than the Eye Can See* - Erik Weihenmayer and Nick Sullivan
- *Bird Dream: Adventures at the Extremes of Human Flight*, Matt Higgins - ***Beyond the Mountain***, Steve House

(special mention) *The Boys of Everest* - Chris Bonington and *The Tragedy of Climbing's Greatest Generation*, Clint Willis

If you are into motivational books, I believe this is the ultimate reading list. It took me many years and more than 100 books before the list was completed. Thanks to Bookshare I had the ability to listen to many of my all-time favorites.

My special mention book is very long and must have required an insane amount of research. I feel so sorry for Clint Willis because I did not need to do any research for my book. Sure, it took seven years, but I was able to take my time off and on and worked at a very slow pace. I'm amazed by the amount of work it must have taken him. I recognized this; hence the special mention. If you're looking for a longer book, then you should read it, there is never a dull moment. *Between a Rock and a Hard Place* by Aron Ralston is a real example of determination. I'm pretty sure everybody knows his story: the hiker who amputated his arm because a huge boulder had shifted, trapping his arm.

It took him 127 hours — which is also the name of his movie — to reach safety. His book explains his terrifying ordeal, but what I find even more interesting is his extensive mountaineering experience. From a hiking trip on his teens to rivers, mountains and of course, the detail of his entrapment.

Every few years, a new edition is out, basically a new book every time.

Ed Viesturs is one of my idols. His book was my first climbing-related read. I follow his adventures on Facebook as well. His book is one of my favourites because I can relate to him and dream along with each sentence.

I'm a big fan of Alex Honnold and Tommy Caldwell

since they first appeared on the big screen, few years ago on the Reel Rock DVD. In my opinion, those guys own the world — and together, they own the universe!

I'm a personal friend of Barry Blanchard. He was my mentor guide, back in the days at Yamnuska Mountain Adventures. Thanks to Bookshare, I was able to read the first and second edition of his book. Kevin is a friend of Barry's and, while I was aware that they were both on the Everest expedition, their book opened my eyes to the other adventures they were a part of. Because of this, I have even more respect for them both!*Born to Run* and *Into the Wild* are such good books. Still the same style but not specifically about climbing.

Erik Weihenmayer is an inspiration; taking on all obstacles to reach the summit. He is totally blind, and yet, was able to climb Everest. I met Erick during the production of his movie that shares the same name as his book. Back in those days, I was a climber in the background for the production. I had no idea, one day, I would be a fan, because, like him, I have my struggles, but in his case, he never gave up — from Mount McKinley, Aconcagua… to Everest.

Bird Dream is not a climbing book but the history of Wing Suit jumping. I'm fascinated by the subject. Maybe, because I share the same drive and perhaps the same courage. Despite, I skydive, I have not the balls or intention to do it again. Is so crazy, the book traces the history of landing without a parachute. I have goosebumps just imagining it.

Beyond the Mountain barely make the top ten only because it includes more than only climbing. If it were not of those few chapters, it would be a top-five contender. I know, I'm kind of picky! It is not everyone who enjoyed only action as I do. I think I have a problem because it is still an incredible book. Forget me, Steve, nobody can deny what you have done in the mountains. You have the same passion and drive that I have, and I have the most respect for you.

I'm not a fan of fiction. I need real fact, I need to know where I am in the book at any given time. When I restart a book, it is as if I am listening to it for the first time! Be sure to pick any one of those books, they are all excellent.

Chapter 34
The Issues I face.

You've only red about the good stuff, now it's time to talk about some of the bad.

I have difficulties trusting people to the point that I'm paranoid. I had a bad experience in the past so now, I trust only few people. I fight to solve my issues, but sometimes the scars are too deep which makes my life difficult some days. Occasionally, I get cut. More often than you think.

I also think I'm smarter than everyone, only to find out that I'm really not.

One example of that is with the Drop Zone 2016. I had wanted to rappel for three years, but didn't do it because I was not able to rappel safely. Finally, I figured out a way to do it, so I registered.

Prior to the event, I emailed the organizers. I tried to explain them my needs and the extra equipment that would be required for me to do the rappel. They answer me that is not possible to modify the system. If I don't like it, I will need to sit out the event. That totally did not make sense to me.

I went to the practice session with skepticism. Turns out, I was worried for nothing. They use equipment totally new to me, and it's very safe. All that time I thought I was one step ahead of everyone when I was actually one step behind. I waited three years for nothing!

Or how about that time I had a very annoying squeaking noise coming from my electric wheelchair? I went to the store and the guy told me that if I want the proper fix, I would have to leave my wheelchair for a week, and they didn't have a loaner. He told me that I would have to pay for diagnostic time even if it was covered under warranty. My wheelchair was only four months old!

Now, I suspected that the noise was coming from the left wheel area. He told me that if I want the left motor replaced, is up to me but I will need to pay for the part as well because they didn't have the chance to do the proper diagnostic.

Disappointed, I went back home with the noise getting worse. I made a post on Facebook and somebody wrote that the squeaking noise was more than likely coming from the motor and apparently, the only fix was to replace the unit.

I decided to take my wheelchair in to get fixed. That's when I started to get bossy with the store by telling them what to do. I tried to diagnose the wheelchair as if it was a car. The problem? Cars have a hydraulic brake system, while a wheelchair is electronic. Big mistake on my part.

After fifteen minutes, the technician fixed my problem. It was a link from the motor, underneath, in a place I could not see.

This is probably one of the main reasons as to why I'm so defensive: for seven years, I complained constantly about the fact that my wheelchair was too sensitive for a guy with tremors like me. I thought that if I changed brands, my problem would be fixed. Unfortunately, the problem was still there, and it continued to bother me.

For seven years, I was so focused on trying not to crash.

I was jealous of the other guys who played power hockey and soccer. I was too scared of having the ball. That said, I found that I was good in defense, never having to venture a couple of meters from the net. In 2016, on the weekend of Canada Day, I crashed into a gal and injured her. That was the final straw.

I went back home and searched for my wheelchair problem on the Internet. I found the information I needed and went straight to the store and had them turn the sensitivity control off. It had been on for seven years and caused me nothing but grief. Now my chair drives normally. The salesman had only one thing to say: oops!

I believe the last experience will affect me forever. I'm not a bad person, it's just that I have difficulty trusting people. Being alone, I have to rely on myself to prevent me from being abused.

Climbing Machine, Remy packing the legendary Climbing Machine just before hitting the road along the Alaska highway from the Yukon. Photo Remy Bernier collection

Remy one month before his stroke on his honeymoon Photo Jacynthe Brodeur

Canyoneering in 1999 at Mont St. Anne in Quebec Photo Remy Bernier collection

In the winter of 2000 Remy and Sebastien Pilote climbed the couloir in the distance to gain the ridge of Mount McKinley Photo Sebastien Pilote

Remy climbing La Goutte on Mount Rundle Photo Eric Hoogstratton

Remy and cut a big bass. Photo Raynald Bernier

Remy and Will Gadd during Remy's adventure on the Kananaskis River Photo Jamies Everett

Jacynthe and Remy on their wedding Photo Raymond Bernier

The team pulling Remy up to Grassi Lakes Photo Remy Bernier collection

Remy in the water with Camp Horizon Photo Remy Bernier collection

Remy in a four wheeler in northern Quebec Photo Remy Bernier collection

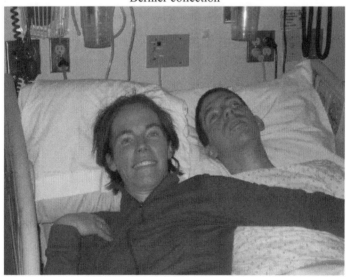

Jacynthe and Remy at the Foothills Hospital shortly after the stroke Photo Remy Bernier collection

Remy cross-country skiing in Quebec Photo Remy Bernier collection

Descending from the summit plateau on Mount McKinley in winter 2000 just before the earthquake Photo Sebastien Pilote

Remy Bernier climbing on Homage to the Spider on Mount Louis Photo Kim Heidel

Remy below the east face of Mount Whitney on his honeymoon in 2006 Photo Jacynthe Brodeur

The paddling team before rafting the Kananaskis River during the filming of Adapt Photo Chinook Rafting

The jump from a plane during tamdem skydiving Photo Alberta Skydive

Carol Page Remy participates in a snowstorm in the Mobility Cup International Regatta for disabled people on Kananaskis Lakes Photo Carol Page

Chapter 35
I'm an Extreme Kind of Guy!

I have no parents, no wife and no kids, so I'm free to do whatever I want!

The irony is I have an ex-wife who loves me too much. I'm talking about loving me like a mother! As if I'm a forty-year-old kid. I trust her opinion and asked her what she thought about me going skydiving.

She was totally against it. She argued that I might break a leg and would have to stay at the hospital for few months.

Good thing I didn't tell her that I was determined to do it anyway! I took the plunge on October 2016.

The jump was awesome, but I was little bit disappointed because I was hoping to be scared. During the jump, I was totally passive, I did not feel the adrenaline rush I was expecting, like during my unplanned wheelchair adventures. Even so, I have to say that people at Alberta Skydivers Ltd did a fabulous job and the jump was very fun. I liked it a lot and it is so cool to say that I have done it!

Back home, I told Jass about my skydive adventure. She was so furious that she hung up on me and refused to talk to me for few days.

That was the cherry on top an awesome summer of extreme activities. I wish I could do it over again!

In June I went rafting and climbing for the making of my

movie *Adapt*. The movie was showing how I could go rafting (with my bad hand taped to the paddle) and climbing (rope ascending) my own way. Basically, to prove to everyone that there is a way for almost anything.

In July, it was off to camp Horizon and the Rocky Mountain Adaptive for a five-week kayak camp.

Horizon is a summer camp for disabled people. I went for four years. Over time, the camp become too tame for my liking. In 2017 they asked me not to come back because I became too much of a liability with my penchant for adventure. In 2016, I was able to hit the giant swing one last time before I went on my way!

In September I went to the Drop Zone Easter Seals. I rappelled down a thirty-three-story building (115 meters) dressed up as "Super Remy!" I was wearing a cape, as well as a T-shirt with a logo that matched the tattoo on my leg.

I've rappelled so many times in my lifetime, that it was just like another day at the office. Only this time, I was going down a real office building. I signed up again but had to withdraw. Unfortunately, 2017 was the last time for the event, but it's great to say that I have done it! I loved putting on the gear and having fun. I have rappelled only twice after my accident.

Another extreme activity I practice during the winter months is sit-ski at the hill. There is someone behind me, with attached tethers, guiding me down the hill. Once I get going, I can barely see, and I rely on voice commands to turn. I would love to go sit-skiing in deep powder. I don't know if that is even possible, but I want to be able to turn on my own, with my partner still tethering me.

Chapter 36
Real Life. Not a Movie.

I'm telling you, the following story is exact and true. These things seem to only happen to me!

October 2016. It's Monday, and like every Monday, I go to YMCA Saddletowne for swimming. I'm going toward the C-train station. On my way, there is a semi-truck blocking the sidewalk. I wait two minutes and all the pedestrians pass in front of the truck.

I take a good look at the truck but can't find a company name. After some time, there's no sign that the truck is going to move, so I decide to go around the front like everyone else does.

When I'm about to roll in front, a car sees me and stops. The truck driver thinks the car has stopped for him to go, so he guns it. Obviously, he does not see me with his big truck. He hits me, and I fall on my side. The car driver gestures to the truck to stop, which he does. The driver comes out and puts me back on my wheels. I'm in total shock and not thinking right.

As far as I'm aware, I'm not hurt. The driver checks my chair for damage and tells me that it is fine. He does not want to give me his insurance and tells me he is sorry, but he didn't see me.

I drive away, and after a bit, I notice that I keep tipping

forward, but my leg rest pushes me back to a normal position. I'm almost at my destination when I notice that I'm driving with only three castors. The fourth castor is there but the arm is going up and down with no resistance. I don't have the insurance info... What was I thinking? Fortunately, it will be super easy to trace because I know the exact address and the time the delivery was made.

I go at the Police station with a friend from the YMCA and fill the report. My wheelchair is simply too dangerous to drive. Paperwork done, I need to wait for the Police to do their investigation.

While I'm waiting, I get my wheelchair fixed. Turns out, there are more repairs that need to get done. It's cost me $500 but I'm not stressed about it because I have no doubt that they will find the truck.

Time passes and still no news. Basically, a ghost truck hit me! The logbook has been erased and the surveying camera was deleted. No name on the truck. Of course, he didn't want to give me his insurance!

The incident was hard to swallow at first, and I had to come up with the money to fix my chair, but in the end, it doesn't matter because it makes a great story for my book!

Chapter 38
Cheap but Healthy.

Getting sick can be tricky in my position.

Recently, I got a fever. I stayed in bed to rest but three days later I still had a fever and was having difficulty breathing. I felt as if I should go see a doctor, but I was too weak.

It can be a monumental task to care for myself when I'm healthy and alone in my apartment. When I am ill, it takes on a whole new level of effort. While it's hard enough to venture out into the world on my own, it was simply impossible while feeling unwell.

On the fourth day I was on the mend until late afternoon when I began to spit up large amounts of green mucus. I was shocked and worried as for hours I expelled overwhelming amounts of thick fluid from my lungs. No wonder I was having trouble breathing. This continued for days.

I finally ventured out to visit the doctor after nearly a week. He examined my lungs and told me he had no concerns and that I should feel back to normal in no time. He was surprised as I recounted my illness over the last few days. I felt as though I had recovered from a major lung infection in less than a week on my own. I cared for myself without support from anyone, a doctor or drugs.

I seem to catch everything that goes around but I feel my

immune system is strong and I can fight it off quickly. I caught a bad cold from Jass after she had complained of a sinus infection. I had a fever which surprisingly lasted only a day before I was back to my usual self.

Being independent is difficult when I am ill. Everything becomes just that much more complicated. Fevers leave me feeling freezing and, with my limited ability to move, I'm unable to do anything but lay around. I'm clumsier and spills are frequent. It's already a challenge to clean up: try to picture the scene when I'm sick.

Another major effort is when I need to do a number two! The transfer from my wheelchair to the toilet is the hard part. When I'm sick with diarrhea, I simply wear a diaper just in case I don't make it on time. Thank God, I've never had a mishap.

I try to stay healthy by remaining active, eating well and by taking vitamins. I qualified for a project offered by Pure North that provides vitamins, free of charge, to all residents and clients of the Mustard Seed, a social program to give hope and well-being to those below the poverty line. They suggest "illness prevention is one of the hallmarks of the Pure North system and ensuring that your body has all the nutrients it needs to stave off illness is one of our primary goals."

I am grateful to have belonged to this initiative, as I am concerned about my health and most definitely would not have been able to afford to boost my nutrition in such a way otherwise. I believe it has had an impact. I take the allotted twelve tablets every day and I get a nutritional boost from things such as multivitamins, B12 and methylcobalamin, probiotics, Omega 3, vitamin C, N-Acetyl-L-cysteine, vitamin D and bone renewal supplements, just to name a few.

Year round, I eat frozen pre-prepared meals. Good meals but frozen. I wish I could have fresh fruits and vegetables more regularly, but they are just not in my budget!

My place is cheap but still very expensive for somebody on government aid. After paying my rent, I have less than 550 dollars left for all my expenses per month. I manage and pay only $175 for my Internet, TV and cellular.

I rely on Meals on Wheels, another social program that provides well-balanced meals to those in need and delivers them to the door. It is such a convenience to have at my disposal. Meals would be much more expensive and difficult without this resource.

I try to make it to a Community Kitchen every month. The Kitchen is also organized by the Mustard Seed. It's a place where six people come together for an evening of cooking. When I was able to get there, I would bring home up to fourteen meals for twenty-dollars. At the Kitchen, I was banned from touching anything on the stove because I'm a clumsy customer. I relied on volunteers to cook my food; I had the job of supervisor and quality controller. We would all share a meal prepared by Karen, our instructor. The Kitchen was really good to me. It was a chance to have quality meals on hand.

Another money-saving alternative is Coco Brooks. Their delicious pizza offers me an alternative to Meals on Wheels. I eat thin crust with all vegetables and no cheese at all. That way, I can eat pizza three times a week and it's actually very healthy and I stay thin. They have also delicious pasta, especially the cheese burger and East Side pasta but I need to be careful of my weight because they are also very rich!

It's good that I have that option because it is cheaper than Meals on Wheels. After buying my "special lunch" (see chapter: *It's all About the "Will"*), I actually eat reasonably healthy for very cheap. I don't care if my meals are unbalanced because I have my vitamins every morning. I have blood work every six months, and I am in above average, even in higher scale, of every single vitamin! Thank you, Pure North!

In spite of my limitations I exercise regularly (see chapter: Athlete... not athlete... Does not matter because I love it!).

I have had trouble with my vision. I have nystagmus which causes fast uncontrollable eye movements which make it hard to focus. When my only good eye is acting up, I see the world turning. I lose focus and my already reduced sight is at most a one or two meters. When I'm in the bathroom, I can't see the time on the microwave which is only a few meters away.

For years I have been taking the same dosage of gabapentin to help correct it. I felt as though I was taking way too many pills. I don't know what all the side effects are, but the list is probably longer than I think.

One I am aware of (and it's kind of a scary one) is brought on by my methylphenidate. My heart rate is very high, never below ninety a minute. But without that small pill three times a day, I'm simply not functional, as I fall asleep everywhere. Not very practical for an active guy.

I made the decision to wean myself off my gabapentin to see how it would affect me. For the longest time I had been taking six pills of 300mg every day for a grand total of 1800 mg/day. I dropped down to 900 mg/day... 600 mg/day... 300 mg/day... then to nothing. But then I could not see the other side of the street! That wasn't going to work for me.

I began the long process finding the right dose. I worked on it for nine months. At one point I went up to 3000 mg/day, but this was considerably too much and, in the end, actually increased my eye movement.

I am currently taking a new pill. The only side effect is to my bank account. It is not covered by my insurance. My doctor and I tried twice to reverse the verdict but the people who make the decisions have said, "You don't have Alzheimer's." They don't understand that I'm taking it for my eye and it is kind of working (so far, all right). That small white pill costs me $80 a month! Good thing I'm taking the generic pill because the original is $120 a month.

Since I stopped taking the gabapentin, I discovered that there were many other side effects that I didn't need to deal with: swelling in my right leg, I had a hard time falling asleep. It also turns out that my gabapentin was the cause of not be able to have an erection for ten years. I never felt the desire of the opposite sex, nor to jerk off.

Now, for the first time, I start to lose trust in my pills. I still have a large number of pills, but I will consider having fewer pills if I can. Yet I think I will always have many pills, just because of the nature of my condition. Yet I try to be as healthy as I can be, but obviously I need medicines to help me out.

Chapter 39
It's all About the "Will."

In 2016, I figured that if I only eat pastas from Coco Brooks, I would save more than $1 every day. After one month, my bank account was well balanced, but because of my new eating habits, I was getting fat.

I was at 185-pounds before I did something! With that new high, I figured that the best way to lose weight was to starve. In only two months, I lost forty-five pounds and I did not put any weight in more than two years. During my magic diet, I was eating half a cup of cereal for breakfast, one Cliff bar for lunch and half of my Meals on Wheels for dinner. Nothing more than that for two months and I lost forty-five pounds.

Off the diet, I eat one and a half waffles for breakfast, one Cliff bar and some dry mango for lunch and a Meals on Wheels or Coco Brooks for dinner. I drink green tea for breakfast, juice for lunch and half a liter of flavored water for dinner. I never feel hungry and I get all the vitamins needed from Pure North. I need to admit my diet is less than ideal, but with my twelve vitamin capsules, my diet is more than respectable.

I'm a stubborn person and when I fix my focus on something, I obtain it, no matter what! I still want my movies to be successful, and I will, one day, succeed.

I have another ambitious goal! I want to be selected by team Canada to represent my country at the Paralympics. It might take me fifteen years but until then, I'm all about boccia ball! So far, I suck but I will become good at it! Watch the Para Olympic in 2028, I might be in it. If a person knows what they want in life, I believe they can obtain it, but I realize that it needs a special individual.

Chapter 40
Athlete... not Athlete... Does not Matter Because I Love it!

At the end of 2016, I started to seriously train for boccia. I got myself three sets of thirteen balls. One set for a specific distance. The rules and the game are similar to curling.

The easiest way I can explain one ball is like a sandbag but round. I have soft balls, for 1.5 to two meters, soft/medium for two to five meters, medium for distance between five to ten meters and four balls hard for knocking.

I train about eight to ten hours a week at the YMCA Eau Claire. I've figured out a system for myself, so I wouldn't need someone retrieving the balls for me. I retrieve the balls in a big plastic bag with the handles through my seat belt and then, I put the balls in a cart. I can easily pick the balls up from my cart. This way I can train alone and for a longer period of time.

I play in the studio at the YMCA Eau Claire. When I arrive, the studio has always been available. If there is a class, I am usually able share the huge studio. So instead of doing ten hours of reclining bike, I play boccia.

After a while I realized that I'm going to the YMCA six days a week: kung fu practice and swimming on Monday at Saddletowne, boccia training on Tuesday, Thursday, Friday and Sunday at Eau Claire and volunteering in the climbing wall Saddletowne on Saturday.

I don't have a family here and the YMCA is like my big family and I enjoy spending time there than home because I can't book any more program.

Once a week, I go to kung fu for about two hours. I'm now sash V. I've been going there since 2012.

First, I participate in a regular class. In 2016, I got a new wheelchair which elevated me up to, maybe three feet so I become six feet tall. This makes me as tall as the big guys. I love that feature so much that I'll make sure that every one of my future wheelchairs will have it.

Afterwards, I have a private session of thirty minutes. My instructor pushes me every week. He starts with a good warm-up of seventy kicks each leg. Even though I have no control over my right leg, which is super weak, there is no rest for the wicked! I can only do half an hour as I'm exhausted all the time, and brain dead from all the information I need to process.

I swim for an hour a week, fifteen minutes of which are dedicated to cardio work (same technique explain in "Roll, roll away!"). I swim as fast as I can for 400 meters without breaks. It usually takes me about thirteen minutes. My best chrono is 11:53. With my fins, I can cover twenty-five meters in about forty-five seconds. Without fins, it would probably take me fifteen minutes for twenty-five or fifty meters.

I also walk on the Alter-G, an anti-gravity treadmill, for thirty to forty-five minutes. One of my really good friends, Lee Mackenzie, has an orthotics business (footjax.com). He owns the Alter-G and I am free to use it (YouTube: REMY BERNIER ADVENTURES-TREADMILL). This very high-tech piece of equipment allows me to walk with only thirty percent of my weight. I used to run but I need to be able to see myself and I can't set up a mirror to see my right leg in the new facility. Not knowing where my leg is, as I can't feel it, is a risky business on a treadmill and so I stick with walking.

When I was living in the group home, I would add time on the reclining bike at the YMCA Saddletowne to this regime. Now, I go to the YMCA Eau Claire for both boccia and the reclining bike.

I also participate in power wheelchair hockey. I love it so much. I'm one of the lead defensemen.

Season 2015-2016, I won a major award the David Donnelly Memorial — the Unsung Hero Award. I'm not a star, I don't score and assist, but I'm a key player as I block many shots, every game. Some teams have a really good forward, my team has a really good defenseman.

Once in a while, I go sit-skiing. Few years ago, I was going at COP Olympic Park (CADS), but I graduated from the small hill and now I go to Sunshine. Rocky Mountain Adaptive has provided me a rental sit-ski. I go with my good friend Jamie, an ex-ski volunteer at CADS. I get way more skiing done at Sunshine than eight sessions at the back of a snowmobile at COP.

In 2016, Jamie, from Rocky Mountain Adaptive tried to get me on board with kayaking with outriggers that prevent the boat from tipping over. I told him I would sleep on it. Then, my weird idea came to me: I could go in a regular kayak, I just had to duct tape the paddle to my weak side. I knew before even trying it that I would be able to Eskimo roll. In my young years, I was all about kayaking and was the coordinator of a kayaking school. Part of the program was teaching how to roll in whitewater kayaking.

Confident of my abilities, I signed up and realized, with the right equipment, I could take on more than just a flat lake. I settled on my new goal of going down the Kananaskis river by the racing course, class II-III.

At the end of season 2016, I did the Bow river in Calgary, with my newly purchased LiquidLogic Remix SP 10 kayak! During the winter, I equipped myself with everything including a dry suit, skirt and paddle. I went to two pool sessions to learn how to roll my boat. Turns out, it was totally impossible for me to roll it in the conventional way. I have a new plan for winter 2018 but in 2017, I'm going on the Kananaskis even if I can't roll. To follow…

A few times a year, I go climbing indoor or outdoor. I have a pretty slick system of jumaring the rope (YouTube: Adapt, Remy's war, Jug Monkey trailer, CLIMBING 2010). Basically, I use a combination of three camming devices that slide up the rope but cannot slide back. My friend Patrick Delaney came up with the system. I just needed to tweak it. I have a static rope (not stretching) to make my way up a climb.

For five years, I competed in sailing. I loved the sport, trading my set of wheels for a boat. I would sail using a joystick just like with my wheelchair. Left and right for the rudder, forward and backward for sheet in and out. I was very good on my own but sucked in competitions.

I made it to the Mobility Cup in 2014 and that was probably the most stressful situation in my entire sporting experience. Because my visibility is poor, it's difficult to navigate what's around me in far distances. Rather than focusing on the race, I became more worried about colliding into one of the other boats, since there were so many of them! I decided that sailing was not for me.

I played power soccer for five years. I was not good at all and I needed to free some time for my new passion for boccia, so power soccer went out the door. ACPSA is governing the sport of power soccer and boccia.

I really made an attempt at wheelchair rugby. The only problem was that I need a wheelchair with a drive shaft that I can control from the left only and that wheelchair cost $10,000. I tried twice with a regular chair, but I was able only to go in circles.

Sledge hockey is another good bilateral sport. And while I knew that it was pretty much impossible for me to do, I gave it a good try. Being unilateral, I was barely able to go forward straight. I didn't give up until after the second practice: I was still going nowhere, but I was really good at going in circles!

Maybe my activity selection is a bit strange for someone like me, but I've learned not to care about what other people think. I enjoy playing boccia, taking part in kung fu, swimming, power hockey, Alter-G and whitewater kayaking. And while it's very rare that I quit anything, wheelchair rugby and sledge hockey were both good ways to learn that I'm not superman.

Chapter 42
The End of the World.

I really thought the end of the world was happening, at least my world! I tried to push my luck with Property Management and it came back to bite me in the ass.

I was given an eviction letter for fourteen days. The main reason was because my suite modifications (chapter *Downtown*) were made without authorization. I think they wanted to scare me... and it worked. I had asked the manager before doing any modifications. She told me that the Mustard Seed would never approve it but to do it anyway, because I obviously had no choice.

Two examples: the door of the bathroom opened right in front of the sink. There was barely enough room to turn around and close the door, so I took the door out. Also, in the bathroom, I was unable to transfer to the toilet, so I added a transfer bar.

My first year was totally fine but not my second. That was just a way, legally to scare me good because, I admit, I did take advantage of my situation. Having lived in the group home system for so long, my requests had always been taken care of. Then once I was in the real world, I expected everyone to adapt their rules and make an exception for me.

I had hit a major wall. First strike: I had decided to store my kayak in my empty parking stall with my 4x4 wheelchair

(YouTube: *Everything is Possible*). I thought that they wouldn't mind if I'm going with all the trouble of a possible world premiere.

Two more strikes came along, and then the fourth strike: before I found the studio at the YMCA for playing boccia. My apartment came furnished, and there was a big couch that I would never use. Explaining my Olympic dream of boccia, I thought they would take the couch away. To be sure, I wanted to put pressure on them and said, "If you don't want it, I will give it away because I will not let a useless couch get in the way of my Olympic dream! I need the floor of my apartment to play boccia."

The fifth and last strike was about my modifications. Word of advice: if you wish to modify your apartment, ask for written authorization first! Handicapped or not. I finally understood and from here on in, I will be a good tenant.

I was relieved when they lifted the eviction because my only option was to go back in a group home. Moving away would mean I would have to say goodbye to the YMCA, Alter-G and the C-train. So basically, my whole life, including this book.

I will never push my luck again.

PART 4: SOME REST FOR THE WICKED

Chapter 42
New Beginning

Just when I thought things were looking up, I ended up getting evicted for a second time. Technically, the Mustard Seed decided to not renew my Residential Service Agreement. Using the word "evict" would have been too negative. Either way, this time, I was told to move out ASAP!

The first time I was given an eviction notice was because I had made modifications to my apartment. This time around, the company stated that I screwed my transfer pole in my room to the ceiling. This was not true, as it was actually installed with the approval of the Home Care Store. Still, they felt that they had a valid reason to kick me out.

At first, I didn't stress out about it, because it was simple to prove them wrong; all I had to do was remove the pole and show them it was undamaged. Unfortunately, that wasn't the case. At first, the rental company told me I had to be out in fourteen days. It took me a month and a half to find a place.

Later on, I found out that the main reason for my eviction was because of the multiple influx of bedbugs in my unit! Seven times in eight months, my apartment had been contaminated with bedbugs. Treatment after treatment, I had to remove my possessions from the apartment.

By the eighth incident, all of my belongings had been moved out of the infested rooms. I even had to stay two nights in a hotel because I was reluctant to put my stuff back into the unit. It was then that I had all of my belongings treated and put into the moving truck.

To the Mustard Seed's credit, they were the ones who put me in contact with Accessible Housing. They did absolutely everything to transfer me into my ideal apartment, including the moving truck and taking care of the damage deposit.

There was one department of the Mustard Seed that wasn't very nice, but for the most part, I had no problem with the organization. I do miss them a little bit, but I have some deep scars from how I was treated, and that will never go away.

Present Day

My apartment is less than two years old and has two bedrooms for all my junk. I'm able to have the Meywalker back (large equipment to help me stand), a huge bathroom with walk-in shower (so big that I can spin around with my power wheelchair!) I have a balcony with nice view on downtown. I even have a full-sized stove and dishwasher.

The management is so nice, and they've given me a place to store my kayak in the parkade for $20 per month. I'm two blocks from Chinook mall, less than ten minutes from the C-Train station. I feel like a king!

And because I live in the community, I don't have a long list of rules to follow. For the first time since my accident, I feel totally free! Except during the winter without snow removal on the street. Downtown was nice for that reason, I never had to plan something according to the snow conditions. Now, everything is planned around the white stuff. Not a very go-getter attitude, but that's okay because I simply love to stay at home now, which is unusual for me.

What is going on? Am I getting old or what?

Chapter 43
I see Bugs Everywhere!

Here we go again. I was free of bedbugs for six months, but that would change after Christmas of 2017 in my new place. I went to visit my friend Vince's family in Stony Plain. I was spending the night of the 24th and 25th at the Travelodge. I was on the verge of losing my apartment again.

I warned the company taking care of the bedbug infestation: take the blame or else, bad publicity. It was such a frustrating experience with them, as they'd cleaned their hands free of the situation, even going so far as to provide a false report. Apparently, they had cleared the cot, stating that there were no bugs left in it. When I took out my pillow during my visit, more than three dozen clung on the inside of my pillowcase. Thankfully there were none on the cover (bedbug proof), since they don't hang out on that kind of material, but they sure can tolerate it.

After my trip, I placed my luggage open on my bed and from the corner of my eye, saw another bug had climbed the inside wall of my luggage into my bed! An hour later, I killed about ten. Went to bed extra worried, slept another hour. When I woke up, I turned on the lamp and killed ten more.

I took my pillowcase and sheets to the balcony. It was during the cold spell of temperature in the deep freeze (-30 C). That was it, I was in total panic mode and alone at two a.m. I was never going back to bed!

I finally decided to call my friend Jamie and wake him up. He came by at five a.m. We put everything on the balcony, including bed, box spring, clothes... EVERYTHING! We sprayed the carpet and baseboard with leftover bedbug killer. I left everything out there for two days. In my mind, no insect would be able to survive those cold temperatures. I slept in my other bedroom, where the bed was so uncomfortable that I never did fall asleep the two next nights anyway.

After two days in Siberian-cold temperatures, I was very anxious to get my room back. The first night, I was at peace. My bed was still frozen, and so were the bugs; it was a hard bed but I still slept way better than the two previous nights. The second night was terrible. I shut the door and filled the cracks, so any bedbug survivors weren't able to make it out.

Treatment #1: Performed on 4 January. It took six weeks to have two bugs getting trapped in the sticky piece of cardboard left around my bed.

Treatment #2: A week later, another specimen shows up on the trap. Once more, I moved to the spare bedroom. The guy could not do a treatment for another week because the previous chemical was still active. I threw most my clothes in the garbage, all my picture albums, picture frames, extra office supplies, old DVDS and WII games, anything that I thought might have been contaminated.

During the beginning of the New Year, I felt crawling on my skin. I was looking at my right leg, I felt them but could not see them. They were particularly active on my head. Could not see or kill. I really thought that I had lice. I shaved my head, but they were still there.

Sleeping in my spare bedroom, I thought that one had made it in to there as well. I blocked off both bedrooms and slept in my power wheelchair for eight nights until I developed bedsores on my bottom.

During that time, I found an article called *The Infested Mind*, by Jeffrey Lockwood, PhD, explaining how insects can take over the human psyche:

https://www.psychologytoday.com/blog/the-infested-mind/201404/imaginary-insects-and-real-problems

That's when I realized that the issues over the last while actually made me think that the bug problem was bigger than it was. I was turning crazy. I slept back in the spare bedroom again for the nineth night and got my sores under control.

Treatment #3: Done in my main bedroom, I had caught no specimens, but did have three new bites in the last forty-eight hours. I couldn't take it anymore. My plan was to pay at my own expense: a heat treatment that kills 100 percent of the bugs, wherever they were hiding, but at a price of $1700 for my small apartment.

I didn't care; as long my serious problem was gone FOREVER! However, I was told that because I had just had a chemical treatment, they would need to wait three months because the heat treatment would react with the chemical to the point that is not safe anymore.

I did not want anybody to open the door because I was scared that the bugs would be everywhere in my apartment. In my mind, I thought that if I were to keep the door shut long enough, they would die. I did not know that a wall was just a minor obstacle for them. They go where food is and they can detect it from anywhere.

Treatment #4: I let the chemical guy do a thorough

inspection. He found only one baby bedbug... in my spare bedroom! After the treatment, I was able to get the renovation for my new floor done right after.

As a precaution, I threw most of my clothes in the garbage and spent a lot of money washing any clothing I had left. I got a bedbug-proof duvet and cover. Despite no sign of bugs anywhere in my apartment, I still felt bugs on me when I lay down.

I felt crazy, I needed some external help! The very real feeling of a dozen bedbugs crawling on me was scary! That's it, I would go and see my doctor the next day.

During all of this, I was taking zopiclone for more than six weeks. My pharmacist told me I would need to decrease the dose gradually because it creates a strong dependence after four weeks.

I decided to take one pill every other day. I was playing with a serious fire. My first day off the pill, I did not sleep at all, and the next day, I had the worst hangover. I spent the day in bed and missed my first playoff game at hockey.

The following day, I told Jacynthe about my experience and she suggested that I cut the pills in half. I kicked myself for not thinking of that one myself. I was soon able to get off that nasty pill.

Chapter 44
It is all Clear now.

I thought I was in love with my previous apartment, but I was blinded by the fact it is probably in the best location in Calgary. I loved living downtown, but in reality, my apartment was a shithole. I was never home, and I was always busy because I could not stand being in my apartment.

For the first time since my accident, I like where I live, and I'm not always looking for something to do. I'm totally fine with watching TV and just being at home.

And remember how I said I was training for boccia? I realize now that this is something I don't want to pursue. I know exactly what it takes to be a high-level athlete and I really have no desire to become one. If I was still on Center Street, then sure, I was ready to train many hours a week, just to not be at home. Since moving, I don't train at the YMCA any more, and I have no regrets!

Boccia was simply an excuse to be away from my apartment and the location was convenient. And now I feel I have found a home to enjoy.

Chapter 45
You Kayaking? Crazy!

On September 7th, 2017 I went whitewater kayaking at the Upper Kananaskis river from Widow Maker to Canoe Meadow, class II-III. Solo, with nobody assisting me on my boat but had external supervising in the person of Will Gadd. Many people I knew thought I had death wish!

It would seem that only James (my friend) and Will Gadd believed in me. Will Gadd is a super well-known Red Bull athlete. Every time I have a crazy idea, he is the first to jump in, including my first crazy idea to climb Yamnuska!

Sometimes, my ideas are too taxing on my helper, but I made sure that this one was a go. I invited hundreds of people to witness my adventure, but no one showed up. Apparently, nobody wanted to witness me drowning.

Since that day, I have become a bit more distant from Jass and her family. She was the first to say my idea was crazy. I did not (and still don't) know why people were so worried! Since the first day, I knew it was totally possible. Finally, a sport where I would be in total control. An adventure where I wouldn't kill myself. Everybody was seeing the river differently than me! While they thought of it as a very dark place, I considered it to be just like the moving water in a hot tub!

And I never had any fear, even when I went under.

On the river, I never doubted my decision. I was ready! As it turned out, kayaking on the river was easier than on the lake. I didn't need to paddle to go somewhere, I just had to let the river flow and focus on the direction of the boat. It was easier than I anticipated. It felt as if I had never stopped kayaking. Here I was, twenty years and a stroke later, back at it! It felt so good and looked so good, I decided to do one of my last movies on the subject, *Everything is Possible*.

I did a few modifications to my kayak. I used it the previous season and was thankful to have done my two pool sessions prior the season. During the off season, I went twice, tried rolling my kayak. Good thing I convinced the lifeguard to not do a wet exit (flipping and swimming exit).

When I tried to get out of my boat on solid ground, my right foot was stuck behind the center beam. Basically, I was riding my coffin the previous season. I did the Bow River in Calgary, the previous September! I replaced the center beam to a full-sized beam, so it would be impossible to get my foot stuck again.

Liquid Logic gave me a very good price on their most stable boat, as well as free Bulkhead for my feet. So, instead of having small pedals, I have a complete wall that I can push with my feet. With the pedals, I had no idea whether my right foot was actually on or off it.

Two years ago, during my kayak camp with RMA, the boat I really loved had only pedals. They fitted me in that other boat with a bulkhead. Not even ten seconds later, I was already turned upside-down.

The instructor took my word for it, and we decided to skip doing a wet exit, as I had already done plenty in my life… He didn't see me doing one. When he realized that I had capsized, he was anxious that I didn't know what I was doing. It took me about ten seconds to swim out, but I bet those were the longest ten seconds of his life! I didn't mean to scare anyone; I really did know what I was doing. They just need to provide me with a LiquidLogic Remix XP 10, and I won't capsize all the time!

To hold my paddle, I simply duct taped my hand to it. I had a sleeve of Styrofoam. The tape was on the sleeve and the sleeve was spinning freely on the shaft! As my paddle was hitting the water, I was able to adapt to every degree required with my left arm. I did not die, and I give most of the credit to that little piece of foam. It also made me look so smooth and in control.

I figured this trick out after my first year of kayak camp. The only downside of my system was if I needed to swim, my right hand would be stuck to the paddle.

Also, with the angle of the blade and the way I get out of the kayak, I can't go on my back. I end up being stuck to my front and end up freaking everybody out, as they think I'm drowning. Fortunately, I will have a new and improved paddle and system for 2018. The maker of my paddle Aqua-Bounds is providing me a carbon-fiber paddle and I work with TOM (engineering students from University of Calgary), every week from October to March, to develop a prototype that will enable me to free my hand. As I write this, we only have two weeks to go.

Update:

I had high hopes for getting a new paddle system, but the prototype remains unfinished and useless. I continue to paddle with the duct tape. Well, this is a complete waste of time, but at least, it kept me busy one evening from October to March. I still had some fun hanging out with the university students. It is all good, and I'm not mad! Just that we had plenty of time for a simple project. If everybody were like me, the prototype would be finished in a month.

Chapter 46
I'm in Love with my Power Wheelchair.

I am one with my power wheelchair. It's my baby and nobody can take control of it without my permission. Having to pay five thousand dollars out of my own pocket, I made sure to pick wisely. And I don't regret a penny spent.

When I'm in my wheelchair, out and about, I'm so independent to the point that is hard to believe. With my manual wheelchair, I'm so dependent, it's like seeing a totally different person.

On my power wheelchair, I have my urinal in a custom box at front. I also have access to every pocket, my apartment key hangs on the joystick. I have a custom-made guard for my armrest, a sleeve for my paper, my iPad on the side, along with my earbuds (headphones), lock and key. I have a fluorescent light to be visible in the dark. I keep a driving glove and handkerchief on hand at the left rear of the seat, as well as my locking carabiner around my belt for my I-phone. I always have various reusable bags for miscellaneous items, including emergency gear. I am prepared to tackle anything life throws at me!

For my quick connector for hockey, I use the same linkage as I was using for my Dynavox computer years ago. Now, my iPad is way, way smaller and I can still do conferences. I converted the linkage to receive my hockey stick (the stick is attached to the wheelchair). Another key feature, but this time at kung fu. I've tied the two independent plates for my feet together to create one big plate. It was slippery and cold, so I glued carpet onto it and added grip-tape around the entire plate. I have my feet almost Velcroed to my plate.

My wheelchair is almost three years old and I've already put 2, 000 kilometers on it. That's the equivalent of going from Calgary to Salt Lake City with fifty miles to spare for sightseeing! Two motors later and it is still under warranty. The company must be really pulling their hair out.

It wasn't long ago that I thought one other motor was gone. I barely made it back home. I lost my baby for three weeks. In exchange, I received a grandpa chair with five-inch wheels. Good only for an emergency, no C-train but the handicapped bus.

When, I got back my baby, it had brand-new suspension. I think they'd replaced every single part! I don't know who paid for all of the repairs, but I imagine it would have been expensive. It did not cost me anything, and I prefer to not know who paid for it.

Now that I've entered into a calm phase in my life, I don't do crazy mileage like that any more.

One of the critical and indispensable features of my chair is the seat elevation. Critical because I live alone. Comes in handy, especially when I need to reach high in my cupboards. Indispensable because I need that feature to get to my mailbox. When my wheelchair was away, I could not get any mail alone. I requested a lower mail box, but Canada Post told me that they were unable to move it at all. I believe that this may be against the rights to make life more accessible for everyone. My landlord has tried many times to have it changed, but the union is firm about it, stating that it is simply impossible!

During my kung fu lessons, I raise the seat and I participate in the regular class, with the able-bodied. I can't do obviously all the same technique, but at least I'm not at midget height. By the way, I paid for this feature from my pocket and it was totally worth it.

My wheelchair is also equipped with the seat reclining. So if I want to relax, or if I'm waiting for the handicap bus and listening to my audiobook, it's super easy to get comfortable — I just put my feet up and I'm able to keep my mind busy with an audiobook.

In fact, my chair is so comfortable, I've even slept a week in it while my two bedrooms had (I thought) had bedbugs. I could probably spend an indefinite amount of time in my power wheelchair!

When I was going out every day, I don't think I ever spent more than four hours in my manual wheelchair. Now, because I've become somewhat of a homebody, I tend to spend more time in it. I really only take my power wheelchair when I go on an outing or when I need to reach high in my cupboards.

I like to use my manual chair indoors because I am able to use my only good hand while still propelling with my feet. With the power, it's simply useless in my apartment since I can't use my hands and can't use ether my feet.

Eleven years ago, my wheelchair was ordered according to the spec design. It did not take into consideration my arm tray, which required an extra one-inch installation. My left arm had been at the right height, but the other was too short.

My brain went into overdrive and I went to work, trying to find a solution to the problem. I decided to cut an old sleeping pad to put under the cushion. It would make my seat higher, but it was never an issue all those years in a group home with normal flooring.

When, I moved on Center Street, I had difficulty propelling my wheelchair. The only adjustment was to make it a half an inch lower on the front castor. It fixed my problem when I lived on Center Street but then created a problem at the new apartment, because it was causing me to slide forward. Of course, I was sitting on a down-sloping platform. I used a book first, underneath my cushion, which was a huge improvement. Then I had an idea: I would make three folds in paper from my printer to create a three-quarter-inch wedge, making a solid duct-tape spacer and reversing the slope to move me in my wheelchair. The result now is that I have a really high chair, but at least I can sit all day! And it's good enough to wheel around my apartment.

It's been a while since my accident, and I was obviously given the wrong manual wheelchair. While I was sure the Government would want to replace it, I've come to the realization that I'm stuck with my wheelchair with the do-it-yourself foam and a spacer. I'm not complaining though, because they have supplied me with my dream power wheelchair. I feel that they needed to for all the kilometers I did so far and the fact that I'm not abusing the system at all.

Chapter 47
I take Control!

At one point, I was taking between fifteen and twenty pills a day. A majority of those were very nasty for my future health. Now, I'm down to eleven. I'm still on ranitidine, methylphenidate and dantrolene.

I flushed baclofen, gabapentin, Ebixa and docusate sodium out of my system. The last one was easy, I just had to replace my orange pekoe tea with green tea.

For nine years, I had tried everything for my nystagmus (a vision condition in which the eyes make repetitive, uncontrolled movements.) I tried different doses, with the best being Ebixa at sixty percent correction. Next, I tried marijuana oil and right away, the success rate was eighty-five percent! I consume 1.1 ml of THC 1 / CBD 20 every day. For those unfamiliar, THC is the part that gets you high while CBD produces only the medical virtues. I've smoked only once 5% THC/ 5% CBD and I hated it!

The THC 1 / CBD 20 is a healthy and natural alternative! It costs me about two to three dollars a day. And while it's not perfect, the down time is much better than other pills.

When I'm out and about, it takes a few minutes for my vision to clear up. Since I don't have a anything specific to focus on, my eye tends to go all over the place, especially with people, cars and everything else moving around me. It happens when I take the bus, and at wheelchair hockey, where there is also a lot of movement.

After eleven years of struggling with my vision, 10 March 2018 was when I made a huge discovery.

You will never guess what I did differently! I simply put on my ball cap from morning to bed! Now my vision is bang on except when I am moving, or if there is too much to see, like at hockey. If I take a break on the sideline, by vision goes back to normal.

So, while I am able to see well most of the time, it's still a mixed result when I'm traveling on Macleod Trail or if I'm at the mall. This may be a time-related thing. At bowling, I've found that my vision is hit or miss. On the handicap bus, it was blurry during the second half of the trip during the day but was fine on the way back during the evening when it was dark.

Who knew that my biggest problem of not being able to see could be fixed by simply wearing my ball cap? While it would be nice to see when there is more movement, I've come to accept my situation and look at the positive. That with the combination of marijuana oil and ball cap, I am able to see what I want to see, at least when I'm not moving.

When I am on the move, the mall is my go-to destination. I enter a special mindset in this atmosphere, almost like a video game, because I don't see people, only obstacles. A naked woman could pass me by and I probably wouldn't even realize it!

At hockey, I can't see the ball in the other end but if there is a bunch of players going after the ball, I have a pretty good idea who finally gets it. One or two times per game, I misjudge the player and when that happens, I need to readjust quickly.

Chapter 48
Foot Issues

During the winter or summer, my right foot always seems to freeze. The problem is that I sweat but I don't create any heat, so I freeze as soon as my sock is wet. Boots, sandals, thin or thick socks, the result is the same. I found the best way to deter this is by changing my right sock a few times per day.

Then, I saw an ad for DR-HO'S Circulation Promoter. This product has literally changed my life! The combination of the Circulation Promoter, DR-HO'S large pads and my new TENS machine worked awesome. It opened my eyes for the possibilities. It was working so well for my foot.

The reality is, despite working for instant relief, I needed to keep it on all day. I rigged a small travel pouch on my belt loop, so the TENS stayed out of the way, on my lap, everywhere I went.

Dr Ho was not crazy after all. The Circulation Promoter worked for the small vessel underfoot. I preferred the big pads on my leg. After a slight adjustment, it was pumping lots of blood to my foot. It was like a big hole in a dam, blood rushing to my foot, supplied by a small creek. It was working but the fact that I was always wired was not ideal.

To help with this situation, I got myself some slippers that go in the microwave, similar to a microwavable bag of grain that you put on your neck and body for relief.

At first, I thought that was genius. After two weeks, not so much. Turns out that the heat would make my foot sweat, and instead of freezing it with cold, the humidity from my sweat created a new problem: trench foot! This was almost as bad at freezing it with the cold.

I tried slippers with thick or thin socks, but it didn't matter. I found that toe warmers worked the best. This wasn't good for my bank account but, it seemed that this is the only way to go. That, or I TENS my leg all time. To offer me relief, I would need a toe-warmers every four to six hours. At almost two dollars each, I would have to become rich quick, or get a sponsor. At one event, my foot was so frozen, I thought I would have to cut it off at the hospital. I did not want the possibility of gangrene to propagate any higher!

Disaster of March 31, 2018.

My foot had never reached this level of pain! The TENS was not doing anything, and my foot had stayed frozen all day. It was so painful that I even lay down during the afternoon, listening to my audiobook, with a bag of grain that I put in the microwave. Using Velcro, I had made a tube and put the bag over my foot. I had done this now for two years, and even that trick didn't work. My foot remained frozen. I decided to wear ridiculously thick socks with my winter boots. If I could not live with that, I would go and see my doctor the next day.

Chapter 49
Doctor's Appointments.

Well, my two doctor appointments did not go as planned. The first one was boring, but still very important.

My second appointment was more serious. I was taking gabapentin for my eye, but it sure did help to manage my foot pain. With crazy thick socks and big boots made for mountaineers, I ventured out to see the doctor.

It did not take long before he made the parallel. He told me my pulse was very weak and sent me home with a prescription for 900 mg of gabapentin. I took my pill and about two hours later, I had a strange heart problem. I went to bed extra early, but I was really scared that I would lose my foot. I was stuck on that thought because of the many mountaineering accidents I had heard in my audiobooks.

The following day, I woke up in such pain that I decided to go to the emergency. I kept the TENS machine on, non-stop. It was the only thing relieving my pain, as it increased the blood flow to my foot.

The nurse at the triage thought I was crazy, but I convinced her of my pain and was allowed to jump to the front of the big line. When the doctor examined me, I had a strong pulse and my foot was warm, but it was also very painful when, normally, I had no sensation at all.

The doctor performed X-rays for my heart and foot.

They could not figure out why I was in such pain. The conclusion was to continue taking my gabapentin and ibuprofen. They decided that my chest pain was simply a panic attack from the ongoing fear I had of the possibility of losing my foot.

It was a relief to know that my neural pain could be managed by gabapentin. I say this because in my mind, what I thought of as a very nasty pill ended up saving my life. My distrust of people got in the way of a possible solution. I was so stubborn, I did not want to be on blood thinner, but I had had no idea at all. Being so severe, my stroke had caused neural pain, but thanks to the gabapentin I am able to live life to its full potential.

April 7, 2018

This was the date of the first hockey game where I was able to see everything! The gabapentin, in combination with marijuana oil, was working above my expectations. I was giving up hope of solving my nystagmus when in motion, and now I'm simply amazed.

I took a few bus rides and my sight was stable. Same with at the mall. If it was not of my foot, I would never have found a solution to my eyesight. Nothing happens without a purpose. I could have been angry about what had happened to me, but having had my eyes fixed, I was so happy, that I had forgotten about all the pain I was in!

Another solution.

For as long as I've been in my situation, I've used BOTOX. No, it wasn't to look younger, but to help me as a muscle relaxant. Then, after using the TENS a couple of times, I noticed that my muscles were more relaxed than ever.

While the TENS was working for my shoulder, I found it to be time consuming. Then I decided to go back and inject just my shoulder, as it was getting ridiculously tight. After treating it for three days, it was back to normal. Now I use the TENS and it really does help! The inventor of the TENS deserves way more credit for his invention.

Here's a trick for anyone interested: put the TENS to a level just a touch above your comfort level.

Keep in mind that if the pad placement is off by even half an inch, it won't do a thing. I prefer the "beat or acupuncture" mode. Every day, fifteen minutes is enough. My leg used to get much more than that since it was always "on" for my foot.

Chapter 50
Popeye arm!

Before, my arm was so tight, that even with the BOTOX, it was out of the question to use my right arm at kung fu. Now, with my super muscle relaxant, I'm using both arms. Dai Sihing (one of the Masters) could not believe it. He didn't think that was even possible! My muscles were very weak, considering they had not been active for at least twelve years, but I was sure they would be back with time. Who knows? I might look buff again!

I realized that the part associated with movement was fried. It was probably still fine, but the signal will hit a road block at my cerebellum level. With this in mind, I figured out a new way to move my muscles. When I want to extend my arm, I'd hold my breath to get it going. It wasn't the normal way to get your muscles fired up, but it worked.

At least 2 x thirty minutes of my private lesson (I did — and still do — group and private lesson) was focused only on my right arm: sixty pushes, sixty pulls, plus stretching.

I'd go four times a week to kung fu by wheelchair. Pretty much the same way described in *Downtown* to go at Chinook train station.

Twice a week, I'd work on my right arm; strengthening to it probably about three times its size. As a result, it wasn't painful to have my arm dangling for a long period of time. I went from twelve-thousand dollars a year worth of Botox to zero within ten months.

Botox is the stuff people put in their face to look younger. I have to inject it in my right side four times a year for spasticity in my right arm, with a focus on my upper body. I started to incorporate it into my kung fu techniques, and also began going another two days for regular kung fu classes. And I still used the TENS every single day! It is in my bed so, every night, I get my session of electrical shock.

Today

More than ever, I love my Indefinite Arts program, and a new season of power hockey is about to start.

Now that the snow is there, I still don't know if I will stroll to kung fu. It's colder, but I don't care. I can always put on more layers. I'm more worried about getting stuck in the snow and/or having my wheelchair break down. With more than two thousand kilometers on my wheelchair, I have been lucky, but I'm sure eventually it will have had enough!

Chapter 51
After October First, 2018
TV SUCKS!

The summer came and now, there is one foot of snow in early October.

Completely disregard everything I said about how I liked to spend time at home. At the time, I was mentally ill and totally burned out. I'm back to my usual self. Now, I say, watching TV sucks! In fact, I only watch *Gold Rush*, *Homestead Rescue*, *Mythbuster Jr.*, *Expedition Unknown*, *Master Chef*, *Wicked Tuna* and *The Big Bang Theory* for light entertainment.

I like to work on other things to keep my mind occupied: my book, my movies… it's like working on my own but for free. Although, I don't think it will be free for too long now. I feel something good will be coming my way soon!

I will admit that I have a serious problem. I can't stop working until I reach perfection in everything I do! This is true with my new video, website, book and everything else I have on the go. I wish all that was even taking me more time to complete, then I would not be in limbo between projects as much.

I've worked more than ninety hours on my video. Most of that was because of my slow computer, but I did not give up! In the first version, the picture was surrounded by a big black frame. Then, I figured out how to make an album and the video had new life. Good enough to give away to a school! Good enough to compete in a disability's festival!

I've thought about entering into other film festivals, but I'm not sure about that. When I entered my video in for the Banff Film Festival, they told me that their competition did not accept slide shows. At least they refunded me my entrance fee. And who knows… maybe one day things will change? It's worth a try.

Chapter 52
Watch out! I'm Coming!

When I was at the group home RIJAMO, I was going at the movie theater almost every week. That was four years of movies. I got to know the lady at the cash register, and she was letting me get in for free! Over that time, I must have seen at least 100 movies.

For three years, I was also an access producer at Shaw Channel 10, where I produced ten episodes of a TV show, *Remy's Adventures* (ex: YouTube: REMY BERNIER ADVENTURES — Sledge Hockey), and the test-piece *Adapt* (YouTube: Adapt screener). For one of Remy's adventures, I did not release the clip because I was the center of the story when the focus should have been on the activity.

That day I went hiking in Banff and I had the Trailrider (more or less like a wheelbarrow for humans, so I was able to be rolled on the trail). It ended up being all for nothing, as I did not release the episode. Upon hearing this, the cameraman who had been with the company for many years ended up quitting! Sometimes, I take my work too seriously. The show was awesome, it just focused on the wrong subject.

Since 2009, I've done maybe twenty-five videos in English and French. I must have luck on my side, as I have not died over the years. My recent expeditions include: crashing full speed during sit-skiing in a very dense forest, kayaking a class II/III rapids. And that's only on tape! Way more in real life, like flipping my wheelchair on a train track.

But one thing I'm sure of, I will be even better at making films, because I plan to make more than one! I'm not talking small production, I see really, really big!

For months, I was totally obsessed, I want to be a Hollywood movie producer. I'd tell you what it is, but I'm too far into this project to be giving the job to somebody else. I have no control at all if I will be producing or not my movie. It may seem like a daunting task, but I'm not scared or intimidated by the idea! The reason is probably because I have all the frames figured out.

I truly believe that my movie will be by far the best in its category. I have a special twist that is huge! Mega! You can try all you want, but you'll never guess!

My movie is super simple! I have never seen a movie like it myself, but the concept makes total sense. I am able to write all the text in half a page. The music track takes lot of room. First, I used the best music I could find on the Internet. It took me three months at fifty hours a week to get the best music track. I probably watched about four hundred videos on YouTube, then for the last half, I used a remix from *Linkin Park*. The song version was totally new to the public. I can say it freely because, I have a copyright for a lifetime, in all countries, on the song's track.

I can't give you any more hints, but I invite you to listen the little preview on my site (be quick because it won't be long before a company ask me to take it out). https://www.nevergiveup.online/movie

Chapter 53
Medley

I go still at the YMCA for swimming once a week. I started to wear my glasses in the water. I'm extra careful to not splash. I try to stay away from kids playing in water. All those precautions are because, without glasses, I can see only about two meters ahead of me. I had a huge watch (sailing watch for those who are familiar) that I was wearing because I could just barely see the big clock for timing my laps. Any other regular-sized clock is just a circle on the wall. Saying this, I actually don't do time trials any more. I must be getting old.

Being trapped in my apartment during the snow months, I rely ninety-nine percent on Walmart delivery for food. About every three months I go to the grocery store to get eighteen cans of frozen grape juice.

Side note: since the event that lead to my arrest, I stay far from food products with high acidity content. That means no orange juice for me anymore!

When it's possible, I get milk at Chinook mall. When this is not possible, my friend Jamie brings me milk.

And even though I don't live at the Mustard Seed any more, I still qualify for free vitamins from Pure North. I'm in a program where they take blood work every six months, and I get a consultation with the doctor. They supply me with all the vitamins I need, and I keep on top of my health with mandatory check-ups. I'm becoming a health freak, always asking my doctor if a pill is bad for me. I consider them all bad but make an exception for those that are essential in my situation.

I don't have my awesome caregiver any more. It's little bit complicated but I will only know next summer if everything was worth it or not. At least now I have someone who does her job and that is all I can ask for. This change gave me the possibility to move my home care days, so I am able to go to more kung fu. I would never, ever switch my days again at the risk of losing her.

Since this change, I go to kung fu club on Fridays. This is a regular able-bodied class. I also continue to go to private class to work on strengthening my right side.

I am able to now walk behind my wheelchair. I don't know if the Government will buy me a walker but even if they don't, that won't stop me! I put on my climbing helmet and transfer belt. I stand with a tripod cane, with help of someone to keep my balance while another person steadies my wheelchair in front of me. I pushed my wheelchair, on manual, for about thirty to fifty steps. Sometimes, I go solo and sometimes I have somebody with me, especially when I'm wiped out from kung fu.

Since Christmas, I have been under a lot of pressure. In my mind, I wanted to have my book finished after my "Drive for Paralympic" cross-country adventure, but it's simply too long to wait. I started this book seven years ago and I believe there is still plenty of material to make it a great book. I truly believe that now is the right time to get the ball rolling and let it do its own thing. I hope to gain respect through the message in my book, and help people understand what I'm truly capable of!

Now, to share with you my biggest challenge yet! My focus has been directed at something very important to me. I will leave behind my comfortable oasis for a few months, to start my journey across Canada on my electric wheelchair. I will begin the preparation process next year, and my goal is to hit the road in 2023.

Chapter 54
THE FUTURE...

I'm sure, I will have a bright future. If I get a movie deal, I then will have enough cash to buy a condo in Canmore, a van for traveling and afford a private caregiver. I plan to give a lot back through my foundation "Disabilities Can Do Great Things."

I want to sit-ski in deep powder. sixty centimeters at least. Since my crash in the trees, I wear a full-face speedbike helmet. If I use an Avalung, my chances of surviving a crash are excellent. If I had an open helmet, I would die suffocated from the face shot and crashing... I would be history, but my mask is fully closed. The Avalung gives the person who is buried more oxygen and an increased time window for rescue.

    https://www.blackdiamondequipment.com/en_CA/skiing%2Favalung/avalung-ii-sling-BD150011_cfg.html

    I don't know if it is possible, but eventually I would also like to turn on my own as I ski.

    I will try to Eskimo roll my kayak for the third winter. This season, I will try a different approach by doing sit-ups in my bed few times a week. My right arm is getting stronger and I'm more determined than ever to get it back to as close to normal as possible. In my mind, it's now or never!

Now, it takes HUGE balls to write what I'm going to write, but I feel that nothing can stop me, and I don't care about what people may think:

There is someone very special to me. I'm in love, and I'm pretty sure she feels the same way about me! Unfortunately, it seemed to be an impossible love, as she was my caregiver. I could not believe how well it was going. That said, I preferred to let her go than be a prisoner of that role of caregiver. I also knew that my book was coming out, so I wanted to scare her away for good to give me more time to finish my book. I felt like mixing love stories and writing will not be good! Not wanting to lose her in the future, I came up with a plan.

Putting all of my hesitations aside, I asked her to marry me! We worked so well together, and I hope that one day I will get her back. I lived extraordinary moments with you. I'm a dreamer, and I want the dream to be a reality! I mean every word I said to you! I realized that it was a practice run but was ready to tie the knot as soon as possible. And just so you know, I'm still waiting for an answer.

Part 5
WARNING: WEIRD STUFF AHEAD

Chapter 55
The Mutants are Here!

This part is an add-on at the last minute. I was going to keep that for myself but people may think I'm more a weirdo than anything else and I seek to be included, not to be judged by my loved ones.

You must think, who is that kid (because in my mind, I'm still a teenager)? A genius or what? Hell no, I'm not a genius, but I need to say that something happened with my stroke and my therapy afterward.

I will explain my mutation and then, will provide many, many reasons and explanations. No matter what, I'm done pretending to be dumb or lie to everyone. My connection with my brain and my cerebellum was altered during my stroke. Nothing is wrong with my mind; the faulty part is my cerebellum. The relationship between my artistic sense and thinking were pretty damaged. With the plasticity of my brain, I looked outside the box to get the communication back. That is why I wasn't able to dream at all the first few years, and afterward, I became a dreaming machine. I'm listening for a few hours a day to the same books. I love the Access trips every day. It does not matter if it is thirty minutes or three hours. I'm watching all the time adventure films. I'm a heavy user of that new path, and that became unreal. Other stuff, I'm still dumb like I was before my accident, not the smartest cookie out there! I bet when it happened, my brain was fully developed; I had control of feeding one type of input driven by my books, I found a new path. I don't know how I can think of stuff like that because it is tough to believe that a disabled person thought that on his own.

I'm sharing this because I'm starting to get fed up to have doors close because people think that is not possible. Because I need to keep my secret to myself, I need to lie, for now, a couple of years, to my ex-wife. Because my ex-caregiver doesn't want to talk to me, she probably thinks that I'm a weirdo, no future and will be on Government Aid all my life. I opened up, and that came biting me back in the ass. We never fought, but she still wants to kill me. From my side, it was the normal thing to do, and from her side, I'm crazy. I still think we will have a life together, but for now, I leave her alone. When she is ready, she will contact me.

Chapter 56
Don't Need a Crystal Ball

Crazy stuff, but I can see my future. No joke! It can seem pretentious but is just average at my eye, and I'm not impressed at all. All events are a map in my mind. To prove me right, I will write a few things that will happen in the future:

I will roll a kayak in winter, 2019.

If they believe me, I will get $5, 000 from Arc'teryx Adventure Film Grant at Vancouver International Mountain Film Festival for my next movie in 2020. If they don't recognize my work, I will pay on my own with my credit card or apply for the Commitment Grants of the Mountainfilm, Telluride.

I will win an award for my film at the Banff Mountain Film Festival and my book at Banff Mountain Book Competition.

I will win an award at Mountainfilm (Festival in Telluride, Colorado).

I will be with my love.

I will have a movie and an Oscar within five years.

I will be working on my second movie.

I will break the Billboard with the first and second music track.

I hope somebody will check back in five years. I can say,

that is pretty accurate. Maybe, I can't see the future, but I'm so, so determined that I will put all my energy toward those goals, and I have plenty! Those goals are pretty ambitious, but to me, I see them as pretty standard things to do. I'm the least pretentious guy around, nobody knows or realized all my mountaineering I did before. Because there are better things to talk about than bragging about yourself, I believed and believed, that has been my motto all my life.

Chapter 57
Outside the box!

I even surprised myself sometimes. I don't even know how I think about most stuff. Every time, I come up with a weird solution.

About eight years ago, I crashed in a sit-ski and broke my helmet. I needed to find a replacement. I had in mind a full-face helmet with a visor but it needed to be easy to put on, so I looked on eBay and found a brand-new speed bike helmet with the front that lifts. As a bonus, it was 25$ US (40$ CAN by the time it was shipped). So, I found my helmet easily, and I would not exchange it, even today for a fortune.

There is absolutely nothing conventional about my movie. As far as I know, there is nothing available that will compare to it. I'm strict; there is absolutely nothing that can be changed. I refused anybody except me to produce the movie.

When I was at the 1010 Center, I felt all smart to think about all the modifications, including the laminated floor on the wall and removing the bathroom door and replaced with IKEA shower curtains.

I have countless things that are used "out of the box" around me. I could write another book on the subject but visit the section *Trick living* in the community on my website.

Perseverance: I think I'm one of a kind when it comes to

a challenge. I get right to business:

Do you think it is reasonable to write a book with only one finger?

Spending ninety hours on a video that is not to standard, because I have a piece of junk for a computer. Too bad if festivals don't like it, it is still a story well showcased.

I spent 200 hours over three months working on the different music tracks of the movie *Never Give Up*!

Determined to use both hands at kung fu. I'm working on it since June 2018. I'm making minuscule progress but the progress is there. I'm still trying to open my hand palm up. It will be quite the euphoria if I get it.

I am training every week walking for nine years on the Alter-G (antigravity treadmill).

Probably everything I do is because I have only one good hand and rarely, do I need help.

Chapter 58
Art

I do crafts for eight years. I was not very good at first, but now, I'm quite good at putting to shame the able-bodied. There is nothing more persuasive than pictures.

For my first few years, I was doing leather works because it was the only thing that I can do whilst avoiding disaster with other projects.

Art by Remy in 2015 Photo Roxanne Taylor

Chapter 59
Age

I feel like I am still a teenager. Even though I'm getting older, I'm improving even more. I improve more every day than I'm getting old. So since my stroke, the time stopped, and I'm still the same kid. I felt already like a teenager when I was at twenty-seven so let's say I'm still a teenager at heart. The best example of that is I still like very, very much Punk music. My favorite songs are still the same ones I was listening to when I was fifteen years old. I'm still listening to NOFX, Lagwagon, Pennywise, Face to Face, No Use For A Name... I bet there are few forty-year-olds listening to that teenager's music.

Chapter 60
Music

Yes, I'm a fan of Punk, but I'm more a fan of folk/alternative like the Lumminers, The National, Jack Johnson, Milky Chance, Hozier and my all-time favorite: *La Chambre* from Jean Leloup. I'm serious about my music. So serious that I listen to it at least two hours every day! I go to bed around ten and sleep by midnight. In my bed, I'm getting TENS, do my set-ups and listening to music. I don't know the names of songs or their lyrics but I know, for sure, the band, group or singer. The bands that I name are just a tiny figure out a much more complex playlist. For example, take the music of Never Give Up! For my second movie, I have already, more so, the music track. I enjoy listening to music more than watch TV. Talking about the film, I don't feel comfortable running the show for part two. I will be happier if I'm the second or third man. Not like the first *Never Give Up!*, the second movie is more like a real movie, way, way more room to experiment. I know it is going to be a love story, the big picture but for the detail, is up to the producer.

On most evenings I'm in my music and don't watch TV. The TV is right for lite entertainment, and music is for a way, way more complex hobby! Most people watch TV, but I can not attend a considerable amount, so music is my number one and TV my number two.

Chapter 61
Marijuana

I use CanniMed oils. I'm a beginner, and maybe everybody experiences the same thing, but I think I'm reacting differently. Since I'm a thinking machine, I can barely sleep. I started to take 0.8 ml of 10:10 to help for relaxing. I realized at the beginning, if I have my eyes close, I experience the best trip. If I keep my eye open, I feel nothing. If I start thinking, no matter if my eyes are closed or open, I feel nothing, and I could not sleep at all even with a more significant dose of 0.8ml of 18:0.

At the start of my experimentation, I was getting eye close, a significant high but as soon I opened my eye, I felt normal, and I was just on 0.8ml of 10:10. I include my experience because I think it is unique and funny:

The first time, I was conscious of everything but thought my body was asleep. I thought I was the only one feeling this but realized, after a couple of days, that I was simply stoned.

A week later, that was just too cool; I increase the 10:10 at 2 ml. I listened to Punk music so as not to fall asleep. My senses exploded, and I started to think, I'm Indiana Jones, and I entered a room full of mummies. One mummy tried to open my chest to get my heart. I was already blown away by the sensibility of my senses. I felt pressure and five fingers over my heart. I said to myself that is insane, I felt pressure and thought it was my mind tricking me. A few minutes later. I put my left hand over my heart to feel my chest. My left hand came on top of my right hand, and then, it occurred to me that the mummy wasn't trying to open my chest, but it was merely my right hand. I already don't feel anything on the right, but it sure moves a lot with kung fu.

It was getting late and wanted to lower the volume of my music. No joke, it was already at the minimum. The next day, I could not even hear it, and the night before, I thought it was too loud.

Next, comes the peak with something I did not like at all. My trip was so, so promising but it came downhill pretty quick. I started to feel one, two, five and ten bedbugs on my right side. I panicked and opened my eye. Everything went back to normal, the bedbugs were gone, and I could not fall asleep all night.

Back at the beginning, being a total beginner, I asked my best buddy to try it out. He won't be happy to read this, but he is kind of a pothead. What was to him a small dose was a big one for me. I rode the transit completely stoned. At least, I was not speaking like high people. I swear if there is one person high on a train, that person gravitates toward me for small talk. Only high or drunk people do that, and that is annoying to me. Sometimes, I wish to be like everybody else, to blend in.

The second time I smoked THC was at Wilson Watson lodge. I was at kayaking camp, and I did not sleep for a couple of nights. My friend was smoking before bed. I decided that I wanted to sleep finally and smoke with him. I think I had only two or three puffs. Before I was in bed, I was stoned. So wasted that I did not trust myself to transfer, so I slept in my wheelchair. Finally, I was way, way too high to sleep. I saw the night spinning away. The following day, I so, so felt terrible. Not because I smoke but because I did not sleep.

My body reacts in a very, very strange way to CBD. I found a considerable difference between the same quantity of 18:0 and 10:10. I think it's what everybody feels with the 18:0 but something weird happens with the 10:10. I feel as if I am at a boring party with the 18:0 and I'm at a rave with the 10:10. I get more stoned if I take more with the 18:0 but not with the 10:10. I see a slight difference between 0.8 ml and 2 ml of 10:10. The buzz is as well small or more significant quantity. It seems like I'm only stoned when I close my eyes. When I open my good eye, everything is like normal, and my eye is so straight. Usually, my eye is going all over the place by midnight.

Everybody knows by now that I have a very complicated case of nystagmus. I said earlier that my problem was fixed with gabapentin and marijuana. Well... it was for a brief period. The gabapentin started to react with my marijuana oil. I'm back to thinking it is a very, very, very nasty pill. Story short, I blacked out twice on Lyrica (similar pill to gabapentin). I stopped taking that pill entirely three months ago. Not a joke, I wasn't able to have an erection. I started to have significant leaks of urine. I was just about to go on diapers when I blacked out for the first time. Lucky me, I caught it and discontinued it. Conclusion: I tried every single pill and nothing come close to marijuana. I take now 0.6 ml of 18:0 and 1.5 ml of 1:20 for bedtime and 2 ml of 1:20 in the morning. I don't have the $280 a month that is costing me so I pay with plastic and will figure something out later.

Chapter 62
I got rob!

I'm the wrong bear to try to mess with! I'm pissed off. I did not plan at all to finish my book on the wrong note, but I can't help it. Vancouver International Mountain Film Festival did not judge me! Despite the fact that I received two confirmations that they would give me news by the end of January. After two weeks in February I grew confused, so I wrote to them, and I came to a shocking conclusion. Who would miss my application after sending me two confirmations? Maybe it was lost, but something important like this and the reputation of the Festival make me believe my application was lost because I have a set of wheels and they don't take me seriously. The thing they would know if they had read my package is that I plan on doing my film for all schools in Canada and the US. That means many students will see my movie years after years. I had a video demo made up with the four last minutes showing clearly my intention, and it is crazy good. I was a little bit worried that might happen, and I chased them to give me confirmation. Once they received it and confirmed, I felt confident and not too stressed because there is simply no way that somebody will offer more visibility for Arc'teryx and do a better overhaul film. I applied for the Arc'teryx Adventure Film Grant of $5000 toward producing the movie of my dream! All the time

I spent over eight years did not matter anymore because that would be things of the past; a brand-new horizon was awaiting!

Moreover, I'm still waiting! I was hoping to get the grant to showcase my story, get the word out and get my book to publication without pushing it. It seems like all my actual life depends on having the grant. I hate so much selling myself this, and I try to avoid it. There is no one out there that will read my book or watch my movie and give me a chance.

I think I'm pretty much burning a bridge with the Festival, but I don't care. Next time that will teach them to treat everyone on the same level. Also, by the way, they are not answering my emails.

Everything is on hold. I need to wait for Mountainfilm, Telluride and pray for them to take my movie. Later on, in June, the registration opens for their version of the grant. I will apply but will make sure they will judge me. I don't know how I will do that, but this is my last chance.

As a first step, I quit my Homecare and get my love back. I'm already taking a shower every day alone. I always pretend that I can't shower but I've still been able to do so. The only way to get somebody from Homecare to clean up and get laundry done is to get showers. I take one shower a day because of my right foot, which freezes otherwise. It is the only way possible, for more than two years, I tried and tried every possible way. I even tried aluminized tread with aerospace fabric technology socks.

I use Drysol (liquid and you need to apply a little bit) to stop my sweating from my right foot. I've been working a lot of trial and error to come up with a solution, get the only pair of shoes and socks possible. I fix my problem, and I have no more the frozen sensation, finally, after more than two years. For shoes, I wear The North Face women's Thermoball Traction Bootie (women's because they are way warmer than the men's) with, after trying every possible sock, Wigwam Ultimate Liner Pro Socks. I spent a little fortune in socks. They are about $30 for the merino socks, but I found a cheaper and better sock in the Liner Pro. First, I wanted to avoid taking a shower, but the amount of Drysol was insane and not reliable at all. Now, my foot is never frozen. Finally, I found a way to have a healthy life.

Every day, before breakfast, I step in the shower. Because I have a busy schedule, I need to make sure that I don't take much time, I listen to the music tracks of Never Give Up! I know by the songs, how much time is taking me. It's like if I have a watch, but I don't. Also, it is a better trick than look at the time every five minutes.

So far, I'm the same guy but I hope, shortly, I will get some recognition from the public and start working on the second phase of the project. I'm still a no name, but I hope to fix that shortly.

Chapter 63
Nobody Wants my Movie

I don't quite understand; nobody wants my movie! I received a letter from Mountainfilm (Telluride) saying best luck for next time. After investigation, I found out that they didn't judge me at all. So far, out of five festivals, I got a refund from Banff Festival and four that didn't even judge me. Vancouver International Mountain Film Festival did not judge me, ask for my money and refused to email me. Memorial Maria Luisa (Spain) didn't judge me, but after an email, they will show my movie. Picture this… film festival didn't judge me, but I don't care because it is free. Mountainfilm didn't judge me, but after an email, they gave me a particular treatment, they are judging it and give me the news one week after everybody. Knowing that somebody will watch it, I was sure that I would get selected, but sadly, they didn't. I guess I will need to get my movie out with this book, I worked so, so hard that I don't want a complete washout. It is one thing not to judge my movie but is pure discrimination to not judge me for the Arc'teryx Adventure Film Grant of $5,000.

Chapter 64
🎵🎵 The Mutants are Dead 🎵🎵

That is the biggest lie! So unbelievable but so, so realistic that even myself I was convinced. It came down after the sad news from Mountainfilm. My movie is a joke after all! After the analysis of my film, it came down; I'm sick, I have a psychological issue. I had two periods where I was not myself. The first one was after Jass, dumped me, and I did all those crazy expeditions. Then, I married Jass, and everything went normal. The second and more critical came after my stroke. Until yesterday (04-10-2018) I thought that I was healthy. Now that I know, I looked back at my life and holy smoke, I'm terrified. All my life, I thought that doing McKinley in the winter was not a big deal at all. I don't know what to think, luck or skill? After McKinley, I should be dead!

After my first episode I was so, so down after the love of my life was over. I envision myself as the K2 (film) character. I started to do all those crazy things and had couples hook up with women. I had that "fuck friend" that had huge boobs. I had no attachments and enjoyed seeing her crush after she started to fall in love with me. I'm such an evil person, I was a total jerk.

The second one (just out of it) came with my stroke, more in the last four years (when I went on my own) but was there from the beginning of my stroke starting with my suicide attempt. All the time I thought that nobody would understand me, I was utterly alone, and the only way I will get recognition is if I selected at a movie festival. I was locked on that idea, but everybody else tried to persuade me to forget about movies so I kept it at a secret, and I worked on my films for the last two years, and nobody was aware. My movies + my audiobooks + adventures film + my book + my website + my arts + my music = my brain was overloaded, which created the condition that I was stuck in.

After talking with Dai Sihing (a kung fu master), I realized that I should tell myself what I am and don't worry about the opinion of others. I'm getting sick because I don't want to rock the world of others. I said before I think that I am smarter than everybody, but I refuse to be categorized as a genius. This statement is a lie because it's true that I am smarter than everyone but probably the dumber of all the artists. Ask me anything, and you will see right away that I'm not a genius. I like kung fu so much because people over there don't judge, everybody is included disability or not. I'm working on my right arm. I suck, but I'm super determined to be, one day, better. I'm the weirdo in a wheelchair who does not care about what people think. In the real world, people judge so much that I need to look good even if nobody knows me.

During the peak of my madness, I came up with my ideas for movies. I swear, I'm a thinking machine. I came up with two Hollywood movies, *Remy's Life* and *Remy's Life — School* (my next movie with a grant) and two music tracks in six months. I cannot explain why and I hate having questions without an answer.

I was so scared of the opinion of others that my eye jumped all over the place. The status of my foot was critical. Now, I'm not so bothered since my revelation. My eye and foot are doing way better. I even, put this morning, my shoes at kung fu. My eye is finally way, way better. All my problems were from fear of what people may think. Perhaps all my problems come from a very, very long time ago at elementary school where I was bullied. Since that period, I feel awkward in a group.

You guessed it, no more audiobooks and music from my movie *Never Give Up!* The last thing that I made when I was sick is a playlist with Amazon. I have seventy-one songs that form an incredible playlist. I can listen for hours, and I will never get bored. I have no idea how I came up with that playlist. All seventy-one songs are equally super good. To give you an idea, songs from Cake, Counting Crows, Nirvana, Bran Van 3000, Green Day, The Black Keys, The Tragically Hip, Radiohead and way, way more. Is my playlist in the morning routine, Access Calgary and all the time before bedtime. I have a few other playlists when I am relaxing in my bed.

Chapter 65
From Smart to Dumb

Looking at my life in the last four years, it's all clear what is going on! I had two different personalities each of which was quite the opposite of the other. With people that didn't know me when I was able, I think I was indeed myself. Super friendly, energetic, funny and all smart too. People gravitate toward me. With people that knew me from before, I was dumb and not very intelligent. Basically, in my power wheelchair in the community, I'm myself and highly independent. When I'm in my manual wheelchair, I'm so, so dependent! I cannot even take a leak on my own. People need to do everything for me. It is sure tough to shine when you cannot do a thing. I tried to tell Jass about my big plan on directing movies in Hollywood, but I never got her to believe. It is so unusual that I don't think she got the message. I tried three times to get her to watch *Remy's Life* but was unsuccessful. As far as I know, she didn't watch *Remy's Life*. I'm always in my manual wheelchair when I visit her in Canmore, so she has no idea on what I'm capable of. Believe me when I say that I got stuck in that pattern. Instead, confront all the time, I kept everything to myself and got more and more of my eye jumping and my foot getting frozen.

Chapter 66
Maybe the Mutants are not Dead After all?

I thought that my superpower was gone, but I'm more and more skeptical. Maybe, my superpower is not completely gone after all. A couple of days are past now, and I wonder if I wanted relief more than to face the truth. I start to think I'm exceptional and the rest is I'm trying to explain the unexplainable. I don't see the future, I'm so, so determined that maybe it is not always going to plan but everything I see in the future, I feel I will get it. One thing is for sure, I was average before, and I noticed a huge, huge jump in my ability to make art four years ago. What I was doing was very ordinary, until my next was *Yellow Edge*. A fantastic art piece that even I cannot explain or believe I did. Now, my art is more and more amazing. I always have an idea and, starting this year, I have two projects on the go. Two is the limit because, if it were more, I would max it!

I tried to have a good buzz with the 18:0 by increasing the quantity, but I still had a better trip with a low amount of 10:10. I'm not convinced because it is not possible. I think the fact that I'm fine eye open is because I'm taking so little that affects me only eyes close. Determined to have an answer to the question, I tried 3 ml of 18:0 and 10:10 eye open. It turns out, I feel like a boring party with the 18:0 and 10:10. I'm waiting for my questions to be answered with Bud

Genius at Natural Health Services. I'm starting, more and more to believe that I'm unique and also, wondering if everybody is having difficulty in coming up with all the money. To date (04-27-19) this is costing me way, way more than ten dollars a day.

Chapter 67
I'm Free!

All those years spent in the shadow of Jass. I needed to have a real break for a very, very long time. I'm not going to blame her for everything. I hope people will leave her alone; I'm the one who had a problem and not her. Jass is a pretty cool lady, and I have still much respect for her. Perhaps I got stuck in a very, very complicated relationship. Jass is my only family, in Alberta. I guess I was too scared to run solo. Also, it was boosting my already low esteem being around her, and I saw her only a couple of times a year by the end.

 Being in Calgary and her in Canmore, I was free to live my real life. Now with a caregiver in the picture, I need to have closure and stop seeing her because I can't have two women in my life. Now, I'm crazy in love +++ with my caregiver, and I'm not with Jass. Now you know, she's not just a woman, she is the woman of my life. She is the only person who understands me at 100%. Even if I did not have news from her for a year, she haunts my mind all the time and I'm crazy about her. I hope to reconnect soon with her now that Jass is out of the picture. I still believe I will reconnect with Jass, but after maybe a couple of years. Next time, I will see the kids; they will be all grown up. I'm at the verge of crying because I love so much my "nephews".

Chapter 68
BINGO!

It's all making sense! Anyway, it does to me. I realized it last night, in my bed. By my bed, there is a window. I can't close the blind, so I wear a night mask (like a travel mask). I never realized it, but I watched the stars while thinking. I leave a quarter of my eye to see, still. I never, never realized it but my two eyes are open, and I see straight. My right eye has been looking to the upper right and left, lower left. The mask still blocks my right eye, but I could see from my left eye.

I feel like an able-bodied person. After all, I'm not crazy at all, and it all makes sense. I feel smarter than everyone but super dumb otherwise when I speak. It is simple; it is called dysarthria. Indeed, dysarthria definition is "difficult or unclear articulation of speech that is otherwise linguistically normal." For two years, I have been looking, on every clear night, at the stars as if I wasn't disabled at all.

I'm special all right; I see myself as if I don't have a disability, like a perfectly able-bodied person. My selection of activity is somewhat weird for a disabled person, but healthy for an able-bodied one. I'm in love with a perfectly capable body. After all, my caregiver was right to run away. The proof that I am not the smartest comes with her, she knew something was wrong with me but I never, never saw it coming. Maybe some of you will be skeptical, but I don't care because that is what is going on. I never felt so light and fabulous. This morning is a very, very unique one. I will probably never have another discovery as important as that happening in my life. Now I can, finally, be free of the weight on my shoulders. I'm a new man, I'm ready to get my love back.

Chapter 69
Conclusion... At Least I'm Trying to Close!

Now, I can say my book is done for real. Everything in this book is real. No bullshit, everything happened for real, and I recounted my adventures, and I did not add flowers to make it more interesting. Another impressive fact, I did not use any notes. Everything comes from my head, other than making a timetable for keeping track of the years. I remember everything as if it was yesterday. Even at eight years old, cross-country skiing in Longueuil. That was quite the exercise to write this book, and according to the opinion of others, the book would be long dead. I worked in secret (except my ghostwriter) during seven or eight years. I'm maybe one of the slowest guys to write a book with my finger typing but I never, never doubted that, one day, I would complete it. First, I had the plan of just doing my mountaineering stuff but, with the years, the need to keep adding made a complete test piece of my complicated life. Never, I would realize that I had a severe problem. For sure, I was on a search that lasted seven years, and it came to the very last piece of the puzzle. I started to believe it when my doctor told me that he agreed, "You are smarter than everyone realizes." I really was intelligent; I just did not want to believe it.

Epilogue (07-19-19)

Holy shit, I thought that I was a nutcase! Thank you, Alison, for the chat last night. You literally saved me. It was the first serious talk I've had in twelve years.

After Alison left, I started to analyze my situation, and it came to me: this is exactly what happened to me right from day one at high school. I was severely bullied in my school days. My nickname at high school was "Booger." All my life, I was worried about what people thought of me. I was haunted for thirty-five years, and I had no clue as to why.

I thought I did not need to sleep! After ninety hours I finally crashed. The only difference is that I had my eye open for four days. Before that new peak, I was going to bed every night but couldn't sleep. I sent an email to about seventy-five people asking for help and only eight responded. I was expecting way more replies.

Conclusion: people don't give a shit about other people! Fuck the world. I am now determined to bite at life more ferociously than ever.

I have precisely the same goals. I have had way too much shit happen to me in the last twelve years. Shit like my stroke, getting hit three times (by two trucks and car), three evictions and getting arrested by the cops. Moreover, all my movies were rejected at festivals, the Arcteryx Grant and my love is gone, perhaps forever. Then there are the problems with my foot, my lousy reaction to pills, missing the funeral of one of my best friends, and having $250 worth of socks stolen because the carrier left the package at my front door. I've been through twelve bedbug infestations in fifteen months, I've peed myself in public at thirty-five years old and my apartment has been flooded by sewage (waterfall flowing from my counter, one inch of water in my kitchen).

I have a feeling that I have yet to expect the ultimate in bad luck. I'm sure I've forgotten some moments, because I try not to dwell on the past. There are more, but I choose to keep those to myself because it involves other individuals. I think I will see my luck turn just because I wrote this book. It will be more critical than ever to reconnect with my caregiver.

One Flew Over the Cuckoo's Nest (06-09-19)
No fiction here, this really happened to me. I walked into emergency at the hospital by myself, long after I found the cause of my problem. As far as I knew, my problems were finally behind me.

I came to the emergency room because I had an issue sleeping, not because I was crazy. My problem with sleeping has been present since I had my stroke. The right side of my body sweated like crazy from eight pm. to one a.m. The other side is healthy. If I go to bed with a blanket, my right-side sweats even more. At first, I start out sleeping over my covers, but then my left side starts to freeze so I go under my blanket, causing me to sweat even more. By one a.m, I'm freezing, and my bed is a swimming pool. I'm so uncomfortable that it's impossible to sleep. So, I went in asking for help in that department, but the people in emergency completely misinterpreted my issues.

I was locked down for eighteen days.

Day 1

They didn't help me sleep, so I took charge of the situation with what little I could do. I took a shower before bed and requested a freshly made bed every night. With the combination of my finding and taking sleeping pills, I was finally able to sleep. My problem was fixed, and I thought that I would be out in no time. That was not the case.

I don't care anymore about what people think. It's all coming back from my childhood: I was different, doing a not-so-popular sport according to the other kids. I was a loser all my life. That was the old Remy, the new Remy doesn't care anymore. Nobody can tell me what to write. As far I know, I'm free to say what I want as long as I give a fictitious name. Maybe the doctors will need to find another job, I really don't care. Let's name my primary doctor, Dr Nuts and my last doctor, Dr Smart.

Basically, Dr Nuts tagged me as dangerous to others, dangerous to myself and with grandiose thinking. Sorry, but I like my life, even more so after my stroke. I've never wanted to hurt anyone including Dr Nuts.

As for grandiose thinking... well, I would like to remind you that I won a bronze medal at Canadian Championship in cross-country skiing and climbed McKinley solo and in winter at twenty years old. I'm not like average people, so don't treat me like everyone else. If you are not smart enough to see the difference between a perfectly healthy person and a maniac, maybe he doesn't deserve to be a doctor. And by the way, I don't consider myself to be the smartest, but everyone saw it (nurses), and I sure think I'm more intelligent than him!

Intelligence is something relative, and I don't think about it except for this epilogue. One thing I'm sure about is I worked hard to be at the same level as everyone and, now that I achieve it, my reward was to be locked down.

My biggest issue during my stay was that I was stuck with my power wheelchair for fourteen days. When I requested my manual wheelchair, my brain was overloaded. It actually made the problem worse to keep me locked up. My power wheelchair is so sensitive that I need to be in the zone when I ride it. If I'm not in the zone, I will crash it.

Think of it this way: for every inch a normal person moves, I need to think three steps ahead. For example, I think five steps ahead just to take a sip of tea, twenty-five steps to go to a regular bathroom. I think fifty steps ahead to take a shower, and 100 steps to have dinner. If you add everything, I think at least 1,000 times more than an average person has to.

That said; I had to fix the issue myself… again. In the last four days, I stayed far away from my power wheelchair. I was able to wind down finally.

My needs were not met!

The only bathroom that had enough room for my wheelchair was the one in high operation with the really sick and violent people. Even in that one, I was riding the toilet backward (feet along the wall and back toward the front). That was only for number two, because I was so jammed up that it was totally impossible to go number one. In that case, I would have to transfer back in my wheelchair and use my urinal. I tell you, lots to think about. After one week of the transfer, I started to have bruises on my left leg, and it was so painful.

I'm so cheap, my cushion is defective (that is why it's only good for a few hours). And being stuck in my wheelchair, I started getting bedsores.

It was time to request a new cushion. The first time, I rang the call bell four times, paged Dr Nuts twice, and the emergency doctor once. Nobody cared, none of my requests were answered.

At mealtimes, I needed to use the recliner in my power wheelchair to take the pressure off my bum.

To keep my bedsores under control, I lay on my bed, four times for five hours at a time. I could not read, write or listen to the radio (except one day where I didn't have a roommate). I watched the wall all the time and did my sit ups, and kung fu was my only distraction. I was thinking deep stuff, and I never went crazy.

My thoughts are so powerful that there is no way to break them down in my mind.

My last request was a transfer pole for my bed but, once again, it was a one-way conversation. Dr Nuts forgot to tell me that I could get out one hour every thirty minutes. For one week, I thought that I had only one hour per day. When I figured this out, I was six hours a day out for the last three days. I have the last conversation with Dr Nuts forged in my head:

Dr Nuts: "You have a new doctor starting Monday."

Me: "You really think I'm manic."

Dr Nuts: "You don't want to take a mood-stabilizer pill. I really, really think you are manic!"

He left after that.

I contacted my family doctor, to get me out of my miserable situation. That Monday he called, and I was out the next day. On my last night, they gave me a new grad nurse. Not organized yet, I waited patiently for thirty minutes at the nursing station for my shower.

The new doctor sent me home and recommended that I stop marijuana. I said, yes, already knowing that I could do anything I wanted to no matter what he thought. I started taking CBD oil right after. I started with a dose of 2 ml for two days (no problem sleeping) and 3 ml the third day. I was not able to sleep, so I took an extra sleeping pill. The zopiclone did not even work. I found my problem right away. The next day, I didn't take CBD, and took one sleeping pill before bed. I fell asleep in no time. I knew I wasn't manic. I was wrongly diagnosed but was treated like one. I had little sleep in a year except for the two months, when the marijuana worked.

After seeing my family doctor, he told me they were confused because they had a hard time understanding my story. They basically made up my answer and decided to lock me down. I thought that doctors were smart!

I kept it simple:

What: I want to sleep!

Why: Because of my stroke, my sweating!

They asked me a bunch of other question, and my answers are probably what ended up getting me locked down. I felt like I was trapped in a corner. I was not ready to answer all those questions, I did not think that was relevant to my problem. I was honest, maybe a little bit too much. I'm special, all right... but I'm not crazy.

The emergency doctor never asked me the crucial

question: What was I doing?

He told me that they will find the reason for my issues if I go to the psychiatric unit. I wanted to have my problem fixed, so I accepted without knowing what I was agreeing to. I really don't get it, the doctor had absolutely no facts to hold against me. Everyone basically assumed my situation. If they had asked my entourage, they would clearly have seen that I'm not violent. The only thing that I am guilty of is grandiose thinking.

I set the bar for my goals quite high, and I've done that my whole life. I think I'm successful in all my endeavors. I'm a dreamer like the Wright brothers. The Wright brothers had the dream to fly — they were not held back for being crazy.

If I reach my goals, great, if not, it's sure not the end of the world. I will always work toward a new project.

Maybe I am smarter than average? If that's the case, I sure feel like it's become a significant disadvantage.

I've always assumed something is quite evident to me when it's not. The best example is the difficult time at the hospital, as I've just explained. To me, it was so obvious that I was trying to sleep when they thought I was wandering. This story did not need to be such a nightmare.

Another example is when I'm waiting for the bus, and it takes off without me. Even after I made visual contact with the driver and I'm ready to jump in, and the driver takes off. Or when I give directions to my cleaner, only to get a big surprise when he is gone.

Emails are straightforward to me, but so complicated to others. You already know about the vast, massive jump from making wallets to Yellow Edge. In two years, I went from

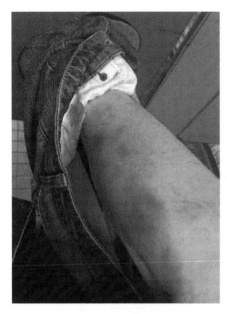

Bruises due to constantly transferring on my own Photo Remy Bernier

Another exciting day at the hospital Photo Remy Bernier

having my best show on TV from WWF wrestling to *Expedition Unknown* and *Mystery at the Museum*. I was a very hardcore guy, and now I listen to only instrumental/classical music.

It would seem that the only advantages of being smarter are the fact I've been going to the pool every week solo for the past five or so years, I'm able to take a shower on my own, and I live by myself.

No doubt, there is really something affecting me. I don't believe in superpowers and miracles, but as of late, something unexplainable is generating my boost of intelligence. I have two guesses as to what the possible causes are:

-The first one, and less likely, is my perfect lifestyle. I never eat crap, I have eight vitamins a day, I overuse my brain when I'm in my power wheelchair, and I need to think with two brains at kung fu.

-That may be plausible, but another reason could be my lousy reaction to pills. Although this is not something new, I believe that it's most likely the methylphenidate I was prescribed for twelve years. It was prescribed just after slipping out of my coma, and the doctor never looked back on me. I don't take it any more and I don't see any signs of any kind. While I was on the pill, I would browse all day, looking at girls in bikinis on Facebook. When I stopped taking that particular medication, I never went back to the page. I suppose that explains my erection problem with gabapentin, acidity pill (peeing on myself) at the emergency, the fact that I blacked out twice on Lyrica, and not reacting to THC.

That could also explain why, in twelve years, I never

went past the fifth ring on my alarm clock and also the mileage I covered with my power wheelchair.

Not knowing which cause is responsible for my mind still remains a mystery, and maybe one day, I'll be featured at the great show: *Mystery at the Museum*.

These days, I sleep like a baby. I'm taking 1 ml a day of CBD oil. Far less that the 3 ml I was taking before. At 1 ml, my eyesight is not perfect but still much better than any pills. For sleeping, I take 1.5 ml of 18:0 oil. I still feel like a boring party with the 18:0 and a mega-rave with the 10:10. I consume the 18:0 because otherwise, I'm tripping out. I have a deep sleep for four hours and three to five hours of regular sleep.

If Dr Smart believes that I will never touch marijuana again, I say good on him. Cannabis helps me so much for sleeping. At least, I found a way better "natural" alternative to chemical sleeping pills. And since I take a shower every night, my sweating problem is also gone!

(06-30-19)

If you think the worst is behind me...

It's been four weeks since I've been back, and I still cannot sit in my manual wheelchair. The problem? My butt was put through so much abuse at the hospital that it is now extra sensitive. I had an excellent system with my Jay 3 cushions. Trying to improve my situation, I bought a brand-new cushion for $850.

Conclusion: The new cushion isn't helping, and I need a new manual wheelchair as soon as possible. I could get it from Alberta Aid to Daily Living, but the process is too long.

I need new wheels and a two Roho cushions. One for my power wheelchair and one for my manual. That's $1500 just for the cushions and $3000 for the wheelchair. I needed to pay for everything. The expensive cushion I purchased is not good and I cannot return it.

Since I've returned home, I use my power wheelchair for going out, watch a little bit of TV, and mostly spend all afternoon in my bed. Unfortunately, my power wheelchair just broke down. Luckily it is still drivable, but I'm kind of scared to use it. If my power wheelchair is out for repair, I fear for the worst. I honestly don't even know how I will manage life without my wheelchair.

All this because a doctor decided to lock me down for absolutely no reason.

07-06-19

Holy smoke! I take back what I said about the methylphenidate. Minimum effect on the short term, significant impact in the long run. It has been two months since I stopped taking it, and I can totally see the significant changes. Let's say, I am more than happy I had taken this pill. It would seem that I found myself a smart pill.

I'd like to tell everybody who thought that I was crazy that I wasn't lying! I'm not stupid. I 100 percent understand everything that is going on, even if it takes me a moment or two. Maybe it isn't crystal clear to everybody else, but it is to me.

First of all, since not taking the pill, I've found that kung fu isn't fun anymore! It has become so complicated; I feel as if I have fallen back to becoming a total beginner. I don't remember stuff even from my first year. My brain is so overloaded that I'm totally lost. Before I loved kung fu so much, and now I hate it.

If I'm not going to start back on my smart pill, I will need to drop kung fu.

Second of all, I packed my gear for going kayaking yesterday. I've never overthought the task before, but now, I need to concentrate on it completely, or I will forget stuff. Making my bag is a very complex task. It is not just getting a few things and go. I need to be careful not to forget my urinal, splint, brace, duct tape, splash guard, life jacket, dry top, water shoes, lunch, towel with spare clothes, paddle and Ikea bag.

Thirdly, navigating my wheelchair at the mall. This is probably the most prominent effect I've noticed. Before, I was totally in control of my wheelchair. Perhaps, so much in control that people may have thought that I was going way too fast, but it wasn't to me. I went to The Bay recently, and I was so scared that I would hit something. I hate that feeling so bad. I'm not my regular self.

I want to get back in the zone like I used to, but it's not something I can do without my smart pill.

I have an appointment with my doctor to get back on the pill. Hopefully it won't keep me awake.

07-14-19

It's been a week since I started taking my smart pill again.

I had to go back on it because I did not want to start a new life with another significant handicap.

Right away, I dealt with my wheelchair problem. I went

to the shop and had the front castor's fork replaced to bring my manual wheelchair back to the original position, which is zero degrees.

I also bought two Roho air cushions. Now, after a week on air, I'm able to finally use my Jay3 cushion in my manual wheelchair. It is such a superior cushion, but I could not handle it. My power wheelchair will remain with the Roho cushion mostly because I need to lower my wheelchair for kung fu and Indefinite Arts.

I had over twenty episodes of *Mysteries at the Museum* recorded. Off the pill, I had no interest, and I found the show so dull to the point it was not worthwhile to watch. Back on the pill, I watched five episodes back to back. I found it so interesting that I had to make sure to take a break and listen to music, otherwise I'll want to watch TV all the time.

I'm back listening to my audiobook and the music I loved so much. I just try not to get so wound up. In fact, the TV cable was down for two days, but it had become such a minor problem because I was able to listen to music and daydream at the same time.

I bought a pair of sandals for my right foot. This is my new footwear. In my manual wheelchair, I have my shoe on the left and sandal on the right. A weird combination, but if I keep my sandal on the left, I bang my left big toe on my wheelchair or the floor. When I'm out and about, it is not an issue because I'm in my power wheelchair, so I wear sandals on both sides. The only time I'm out with my manual wheelchair is when I go kayaking. I put sandals on both feet since I get pushed around.

Finally, I figured out that my problem was not a problem at all. It was just a perception of the outside world.

I stopped my sleeping pill and THC oil cold turkey. I think this is my best move ever. During the first four nights, I slept maybe five times for twenty minutes. Last night, I stayed in bed for eleven hours, and needed a kick in the butt to get myself up and moving.

The fascinating thing is that I'm never bored during those long nights. In fact, it is my favorite time of the day. I could be in bed a while longer, just thinking with my eyes close, resting. I did it for three years, and never went crazy.

I also never feel tired now because of my smart pill. If I need to take a nap in the afternoon, I take it, and that way, I feel like my batteries are always full. Another fascinating fact is that I believe I'm still conscious when I sleep, but I have no control over what I think or dream. I say this because when I was dreaming last night, I heard a dog barking and I kept dreaming.

My dreams are super weird and mostly refer to my childhood at my family cottage. For example, I was on the lake, on a windsurfer board, fishing for trout. I got a very unusual bite. I caught a fish and it was pulling like a huge trout. When I reeled it out of the water, it was small, ugly-looking fish. I decided to leave it on the hook and go to the shore. When I got to shore, I put down the line and the fish unhooked itself and flopped its way back to the water, immediately hiding under the sand. I knew it was there, so I tried to grab it, but the fish escaped forever, and that was the end of my dream.

I really don't know why these dreams come to me. The event I was dreaming about actually took place when I was ten years old.

When I had gone to the hospital, I had stopped taking

my smart pill. The pill wasn't there any more to keep me awake during the day, so I was able to crash hard.

The reason I had stopped taking my smart pill is because I kept watching girls in bikinis on Facebook. I'm obsessed, not with sex but with my caregiver. It was too painful to be apart from her, so I stopped hoping my hormones would go back to normal. That was a terrible idea.

All of the following events are because I could not bear my love any more. I listened to nature music to try and forget her.

Since I'm back taking my smart pill, I have gone back to the Facebook page. I also listen to a lot of The Lumineers and Hozier. Lumineers because I proposed her on "Slow it Down" and Hozier because she likes it.

It is so, so painful but I can't help it, I'm that way now. She's the only person with who I had that magic moment with in all of twelve years. Remember, I could not have an erection for ten years, so now my hormones are getting the best of me. I daydream of her most of the day. I think a good part of the night of her. I loved her so much and I don't see my future without her.

Jass wanted me to forget her, and that is mostly the reason I don't talk to Jass anymore. That and she thinks I'm crazy as well. My caregiver is the only person I have opened up to, and I scared her away. I need somebody with who I can share life because I feel so lonely since I had my stroke. Everything I told you is going to happen. Even the condo in Canmore. I cannot talk about my unique problem to anyone, even my therapist, because of the fear they won't believe me.

Now, I own this world. It's time for redemption. The most important thing is to reconnect with my caregiver. The second most important thing is my movies. In everything I do, I seek to be the best. This is true with my films, my art, my book, my website, kayak and kung fu.

I was in the hospital for eighteen days, and they did absolutely nothing except abuse me. I'm a victim of a medical fuck-up. LEAVE ME ALONE!!!

07-19-19

This is more than serious stuff. Hopefully, people will start to believe me because it is not a joke. I almost died last night!

I went to see my doctor yesterday. I told him everything and he believes me. By the way, he is the only person I was comfortable sharing my situation with, and he did not think I was missing some screws. It felt so good to have somebody in my camp finally. I have tried talking to other people about the big picture, but I was never able to make them believe.

I thought that having an ally would make me feel better about myself. My brain saw it differently. Time was going by way too fast. At swimming, one hour felt like fifteen minutes. I don't recall what I was thinking, but it was deep. I felt like I had just left the pool, but it was already time for a shower and bedtime.

I recall jerking off many times in the last week. Before that, not so much. I'm not obsessed with sex, but with my caregiver. This is not me; my hormones are taking over.

At bedtime, I had the real feeling that my heart was going to explode, and I would fall asleep forever. Of course, I did not sleep but stayed in bed for thirteen hours, just to calm down. I was taking way too much methylphenidate.

From that morning on, I'll be taking half a pill three

times a day for a total of 30 mg compare to the 60 mg, I'm prescribed.

I'm back listening to hypnotic nature music, and this is officially the beginning of the new Remy. I was so, so close to going on the other side. I just did not want to die yet.

07-20-19

I stayed in bed for eleven and a half hours and slept for nine. So deep that I can't recall my dream. I realized this morning that everything in my life after my stroke was an obsession. You know already all about my love, film, website, art and music but there is also the less obvious stuff:

-My food, my vitamins, to look thin and healthy, to be young by heart are an obsession. In fact, I get along very well with people in their twenties. In fact, my best buddy and all my good friends are in their twenties or early thirties.

-I've become obsessed with always buying vast quantities of stuff. For example, four years ago, I bought twelve containers of soap for the floor. I still have two which will never get used because my cleaner uses his own. I bought five litres of dish soap and a little bit after, I was using the dishwasher, so the soap is entirely useless. I buy ten boxes at a time of Cliff Bar. I used to buy ten bags of cereal. I bought fifteen pairs of socks at $30 each. Basically, I never buy only one item. This all started when I discovered Walmart delivery.

- Kayaking is an obsession, but I really have it dialed in by now. Rolling my kayak was an obsession. I did a set up every day for eight months. There is not even one day that I skipped. When I was training for climbing Yamnuska, I did not miss one day.

-My climbing system is a complete obsession. For the Drop Zone, I found a way where I can rappel safely. The only detail that I did not get is that they had the system already foolproof. My method for the pool is an obsession. Boccia was a huge obsession. Being stubborn and not wanting to quit at sledge hockey and wheelchair rugby is another.

-Five years ago, I was playing an online game called Travian eight hours a day. I was so into it that within two years I was the leader of a mighty alliance. In two years, I reached what usually takes people a lifetime.

-My showers are an obsession. It took me many years to figure it out, but now, I can be proud of my shower with only a few more steps than an able-bodied person. I could only achieve it by taking a few more risks than an average handicapped person is willing to take. I will never again let someone shower me.

-I also like to keep my apartment presentable, which is the drive behind having a professional cleaner every second week.

-My biggest obsession of all is fear of accidentally going "number one" for any of my unusual activities like kayaking, skiing, etc.

I tried to do things and not let my bathroom break dictate my selection of activities. Often, I'm with a regular-bodied person, and I don't want to be trouble, for fear they decide not to take me any more. I think I reach the other level of doing my business with anybody and it is not embarrassing for anybody.

-The way I present myself in public is totally an obsession. The fact that I was bullied in my younger days fueled the fire. That is why I always wear very bright, stylish jackets.

-My foot is also a total obsession. One day, ten years ago, I banged my left big toe on my wheelchair wearing sandals. So far, the only possible way was to have one shoe on the left and sandal on the right. I really believed that was the way to go until this morning. I decided to try sandals on both feet. It turns out, it is impossible to hit my wheelchair with my one-size-too-big sandals. I stuck with the idea.

-Facebook and Instagram, especially when I post something and people like it, is totally an obsession. The only recognition and attention from the public I was getting was with my posts. On Facebook, I got an impressive 9, 000 likes. Not bad for a no-name with only 600 friends.

-Email is totally an obsession. I look at least a dozen of times a day but it seems like I'm getting a lot of spam and not so much real mail.

-Bedbugs are the most extreme obsession. Even after more than a year, I suspect every crumb in my bed. If I feel something on my leg, my mind thinks it is a bedbug. As soon I feel one, I feel like there are a dozen crawling on me. I think I'm traumatized, and it is beyond just an obsession.

07/21/19

All the things I see in the future are going to happen because I'm stubborn in an extreme way.

I've tried to be the best at everything. I have a non-profit business registered at the Federal level. I figured everything out myself, and I do the bookkeeping on my own with Quickbooks Online. This is the second year I've run it, and everything is in order, even if I have no transactions as of yet. I had my taxes done last year by professionals. There are still no transactions, however, I believe that this is proof that I cannot wait when I have an idea.

-Having the best credit is an obsession. I have twenty-thousand dollars, which I knew would be handy one day. I knew, for instance, that my family wouldn't pour a dime into my project.

With my credit, I was able to hire somebody to write my book. I pretty much live on my credit card and use my income to pay the minimum balance. I don't care about the future because this book will be out, and I've known for a long time that it will be successful. I just did not know how successful, but I think I will get the jackpot!

This is the second night in a row where I have slept like a baby. This time, I remember one dream, and it was reasonable compared to the nonsense I used to dream. I think my sleeping problem is fixed forever. After three years of no rest, I had forgotten how good sleeping felt.

I've gone back to the mall. It had been a while since my last visit, after I stopped going completely. It turns out I'm still the same man, just not as possessed. I need to go slower than before, but my capacity to be in the zone is still there.

Previously, it was one way: fast and determined. Now, I just need to go a little bit slower, be more careful and readjust my lifestyle a little bit.

Things were very different when I was off the pill, everything seemed to be so big. While I was at a huge disadvantage, I find that it really put things into perspective. Being back on the smart pill, I'm back in the zone. It's as if I'm ready to run a long ultra-marathon and not a short sprint.

By the way, this is my second day in a row writing. This gives you an idea of how much I was able to write in a six-hour period. No wonder it took me so long! Personally, I've always thought that I must be the most determined guy out there. I felt that my wheels are keeping me from having recognition of some sort. The world is not equal at all. Without this book, I would probably just fly under the radar, but I wanted to change that, which is why, seven years ago, I started to write this book.

With every door shut in my face, I have learned to grow, getting better and better every day. Now I feel that it is time for redemption. I should have been discovered a long time ago, but there is no room on the plateau, for a man with a handicap.

Hopefully, my story will be a lesson for everybody out there: never judge somebody by the way he looks, especially with a wheelchair and with a speech disability. I want to change this world for us handicapped.

The fight will continue beyond this book.

I Smell a Peaceful Revolution!

Prologue

Email to my friends on October 25th 2019:
"I'm not a normal person. I'm a freaking chemical mutant. I should feel good about what happened to me, but it is a real curse."

This is a period of waiting, waiting for what? To get some recognition from the public. I've been so waiting for that day for eight years, every time I think this is it, but no, I remain unknown. This time, I was sure that the day would become. I was living on my credit card, no worries because I will see an end soon. I realized that I'm a dreamer only last week with $1 500 left on $20 000 on my credit cards and line of credit. I'll be fine, but I thought that the game was over. I was dreaming about the day; the financial trouble would be the past. Because I will be honest, my ambition is more significant than my low income. I need to have loans to survive. My family is sure not encouraging me and is not willing to lend me money for my projects. The only possible way was to have the best credit possible, so I paid for everything with my credit card and paid off the full amount every month. I started to do this five years ago when I was living in the community. I'm no longer able to pay the total amount. It adds up pretty quick with my ghostwriter, the marijuana ($16 a day) and my three cushions I needed to buy after my stay at the hospital.

I decided to start this book in the wait for the magic day.

There is no point in working on whatever I like. The first *Never Give Up!* is done for about two months. There is absolutely no point in starting a new movie. My website is up to date, and I cannot stand watching TV. I watch only a few shows, and I can watch them whenever I want because I recorded them on the "PVR." It seems that I have a few days a week totally free, so my life is pointless if I watch the wall thinking. I cannot stand silence for even one minute, so I'm listening to my new discovery, "Punk unplug." I don't know why this channel is not more popular. Very positive, no electric instruments, excellent beat and somewhat alternative. All the other channels might be suitable for a short time, but this one, I can listen indefinitely. It is always playing in my apartment.

According to the negative response, in my media hunt, it could be another year of disappointment. I don't know if I have enough material for a complete book, but the worst thing is that the book is just for me, and that will be all right because it will help me waiting. I decided to do something with my life. Writing is a form of therapy for me. I'm slow so that it will take me a long time. That should keep me busy for a few months to who knows.

In this book, I'm whining a lot, and I will give out ten of my tricks for thinking outside of the box. Basically, using to your advantage what is very common around you in a way nobody even thought of before I came along. Some tricks, it is just to know the resource because I only follow the proper procedure. After this book, hopefully, it will be enough to convince the most skeptics.

I seek a better world for us because we are supposed to be all equal, and we are not. I suffered two significant discriminations and injustices in the last few months. The first, my registration for a Grant of $5000, was put in the garbage, and they didn't even bother to tell me. The second, way more critical, was my recent stay at the hospital. I have a speech disability, which makes me pretty hard to understand. I came to the hospital with a particular problem. They had a hard time following me, so they pretty much heard what they wanted to hear. I was admitted to the psychiatric unit, and they did absolutely nothing to solve my main concern.

Having a disability could be an asset instead of a pain in the butt! I'm incredibly handicapped, and I live alone, with no Home Care, nobody supporting me... I need to recommend you not to drop Home Care if you are in that situation unless you are in a significant life challenge. If they are making your life easier, then don't lose them. I am all about making the experience more accessible. For me, they were getting on my nerves. I gamble, and now I enjoy very much living, with way more satisfaction than to be living in an institute or group home. I recommend you to go on my website www.nevergiveup.online and go to the tab Tricks living in the community. I have fifty-plus tricks that I use regularly.

The tricks are mostly for someone like me, but there are some very interesting to everyone. The handiest one is probably my mind-blowing diet. Yes, I will propose a weight management solution that really works.

For the beginning, let's start with the whining to get that over as quickly as possible. Sorry for my sorry ass, but I think there is much to say and understand. I tried to do an excellent job in my first book, but I have a way better understanding of what happened to me.

Part 1:
Whining and the Facts!

Supernatural Shit!

Let's describe my big mess. I like to say that I never wish that. Anyway, it is a science fiction and superhero shit, so it was very far or non-existent, in my thought, until a few months ago. The opening line is for real, "I'm not a normal person. I'm a freaking chemical mutant." I only wished to be equal as my pair, be treated fairly and without discrimination.

I'm a victim and not the other way around of the medical system. By the way, I like to mention before I forget that I'm done with the guilty chemical. I feel way better, and I can think straight and start to sell my art. With the pill, I was obsessed with keeping all my crafts. I wanted to keep it in the case; a movie festival intends to display it. I can not control that so better to start making some money with it.

I don't get it; methylphenidate is only affecting the brain. My brain is totally healthy; all my problems are generated below, in the cerebellum. For twelve years, I have prescribed the highest dose possible of that drug, and I did not even need it. Neither does it work to keep me awake. I'm off the pill, and I still need to rest the same amount in the afternoon. Rest, because it was impossible to sleep, but now it is another question. For the first seven years, I was taking two-hour naps EVERY afternoon.

The doctor gave me that when I was slipping out of a coma and never checked back on me. I don't know if he could but it should be checked anyway, if it is such a potent drug, especially when he prescribed the highest dose.

I complained and complained about my nystagmus

(involuntary eye movement) often at first. For me, that was a massive insight that maybe something was wrong. The specialist should have cut it because he had my list of medications and should know that was a side effect of the drug. My nystagmus was faster than usual; he should have figured it out then because I'm not aware that nystagmus can be as rapid and act the way as mine did. All the nystagmus I found on the web are very different, more significant movement and happened at slow speed. Instead, he put me on a high dose of gabapentin. The gabapentin never really worked. Alternatively, instead of affecting my eyes, it did affect my penis. For eight years, I wasn't able to have an erection, and my sperm (still today) is bright fluorescent yellow. Not that I'm using my plumbing, but I hope to change that. It is quite alarming to see something so disgusting and un-natural escape your body. I always try to be as healthy possible, and that one was and is out of my reach.

After a couple of years of struggle, it seemed that doctors were not going to fix my problem, so I decided that I will find a cure. And I did! It turned out the biggest of my issues is from the methylphenidate.

Since I stopped, my nystagmus is not entirely gone but is way, way better. I swear, but it is acting two hours in the morning and one hour in the evening. Before I had downtimes a couple of times a day, and the downtimes were way, way more violent. In a crisis, I could see only two meters. Now, I can still see five meters or so.

The magic pill affected my eye and developed my brain to a ridiculous level. Like I read somewhere, the brain is like a muscle. Methylphenidate doesn't make you smart. It gives you the tool to over train the mind. Like no one else, I trained that muscle like there was no tomorrow. I bet I have one of the most developed brains around. I was doing the heavy lifting for the brain, and now, it is paying off. Maybe too much because what good does it to ride a racing car when the limit is only fifty km/h? The society set the speed very low for someone like me. So low that it is boring to live. That is why I write again before my first book is even published. Maybe, a typical individual would not notice a difference, but I sure do. For eight to ten years, I've been listening up to twenty-five hours/week of audiobooks. I'm thinking really, really hard for my movies. I write much more than the average person. My favorite past time is doing arts and kung fu. I'm a technology person, and I have my website. All those things require brain work. Perhaps, methylphenidate is having the same effect on everyone, including me, but because I over train my brain, now I have a super brain. But this doesn't take the blame off the shoulders of the system. With all the therapy I did, they suggest always do more if you want to recover. I did more, and that is biting me back in the ass.

I hope I was clear enough on what happened to me, and I hope that people will recognize that I am a victim and not someone who wishes it to happen to me. The medical world should take all the blame. That is too much to ask so it's better to have the small guy take the responsibility instead. They are sure not proposing a solution or helping me out to fix the issue. They are the ones who created the problem, and they should fix it. Instead, I'm the one trying to convince all my friends but it isn't working, and they tag me as crazy. I guess the ones who don't know by now, are the ones still talking to me. All the others, I don't hear any more from them.

Fake News?

I tried two times this round, and I still didn't make it! Everyone boycotts me. I can't get through, but there are a couple of handfuls of people who make the news with fewer things to talk about than me. It is so unfair; I want to have the spotlight on me. I thought that with a piece of news that big, I would be broadcast.

A few years ago, I contacted the media for the colossal injustice I was facing with the Mustard Seed. It seemed so huge that I was a victim, but the Mustard Seed made it look to their advantage and made me the villain in their big problem of the bedbugs. They were kicking me out on the street. It is not my problem if I'm the only one who washed his bed once a month? I had bedbugs almost every month, and they decided to kick me out after eight times. I'm not the problem, but that building is full of bedbugs. I thought that the media would jump on the story, but no. I moved from the Mustard Seed for a way better set-up. I did not realize then, but I was living in a 'shithole'. Shame on the Mustard Seed to want to abuse me. Because it is hard for me to communicate, the fight was lost before it even started. I face discrimination again with my handicap. Never, this would slide with an able body but with a person full of handicaps, a totally different question. They never suspected this would be exposed one day. I guess, now, it's redemption time.

In 2018, I was planning to cross Canada with power

wheelchairs for Paralympic 2020. That is massive news in my book. No doubt, I will be broadcast on the news. Guess what? They didn't believe me at all! I think that is the most significant blow to my pride. What am I supposed to do if people don't believe in my projects? I decided then to push the endeavor for 2024. It will be way easier to get people on board, whether for fundraising and, more importantly, to make them believe that I will do it if I break through one day. It is something I still dream about. I think this is such a cool project, and I will get me out and explore my country like no other way.

I look forward to this day, and it will be a nice change to my routine.

That bitter experience stayed in me, and this time, I will give them no choice but to talk about me. Little bit stress out, I had six news in one including my arts, my overdose, my movies, my tattoos, my mind-blowing diet and my wish to sue Alberta Health Services. Maybe, I had way too much to talk about, but in my mind, if it was not enough the first two times, I am going all out this way around. I did not care too much about spending in the last few months because I knew, if I'm broadcast, it will be super easy to publish my book with the financial ease that goes with it. I stopped just in time trying to live like a king; now, I live the most miserable way possible, but I'm used to living this way, I been living like it for five years. I usually have a nice cushion, and now the pillow is completely gone, and the interest payments are killing me. I'm sure kicking myself. I could have a lovely book, but now I need to pay for most things, such as my ghostwriter and my expenses from my hospital stay. I needed to buy 2 500$ in cushions and to make my life livable, my marijuana at $16 a day. It adds up quicker than anticipated.

Three times in a row, they did not believe me or were simply not interesting enough. Of course, I'm unique, but that isn't an excellent motive to ignore me. I have easily the strongest drive for a disabled person, maybe everyone all together. The news people are not used to seeing a disabled person with so many exciting things to share to the public, that they don't believe me and ignored me.

I reconsider the integrity of the news. If they ignored 1% of the legit story, no could not happen. Are they really sharing what is going on in the world? That cannot be. I guess I'm the only one that stays off the air. I'm probably better to have them talking about me than me trying to get my story around.

My new approach is to do my thing and let the media figure out what I am. Anyway, that should be a short time after I publish my first book.

I had in mind a publisher oriented toward climbing with a clothing company, but this idea was short-lived because I can't get their attention without the news. I'm switching to go the self-publishing way. It won't be free; I need to cash in my RDSP. No matter what, my book will be on bookstore shelves.

More Ink, Baby!

Let's say I got a lot of inks, in a short time. First, it was for my five tattoos' color. Already I've had my logo tattooed, one that only represents me, for a couple of years on my right calf. I got it after a bet with one of my good friends. Of course, I won the bet and actually, I wanted it anyway. He just did not know that. That is probably the most straightforward bet I placed in my life.

My tattoos are all very unique and mean a lot to me. I don't get people tattooing skulls or other dark matter. Probably, it is for showing their toughness, but I have not the desire to express my toughness through unmeant full tattoos. I got a whitewater kayaker, my unique climbing rig, the logo of kung fu, Calgary Power Hockey League and Rocky Mountain Adaptive. I got them without too much thinking after my overdose. I did not care about people after the incident or accident. I don't know what I should call it? I thought that was it, so unfair, I still had everything to accomplished. I did not want to leave with everybody thinking that I was a liar. If I was put on this world for a reason, then I blew it good. I want to be remembered as someone with a unique drive who fights for the condition of the disabled and not for a liar.

With my new window on life, I finally had the guts to do it. I took the opportunity to have a little bit of fun. I posted for my 600 friends on Facebook that I had tattoos done but used a very inappropriate picture, and my amusement comes from the fact that seventy-five people liked it. If they believe that I'm stupid enough to put a ridiculous tattoo on myself, I say good on me. I'm quite proud that I got so many people to bite at my prank.

One month later and I got a new idea. I thought that my tattoos would be seen as a sign of rebellion, but I was surprised that everyone liked it. There is nothing taboo about my tattoos, and everyone is comfortable talking about them. I envision my complete left arm filled with sketches but rather to be expensive and sophisticated. I wanted to have simple drawings in black ink. I gathered pictures of the designs around the Internet. My tattoos have a specific and unique signification. I'm sure I'm the only weirdo who had an anti-bullying logo, a book, a camera video, a clapperboard, a paint palette and a guitar? It took three hours for the artist to complete and cost me $300. I think it is the least expensive sleeve ever. I'm simply in love with my tattoos. Maybe I was missing the guts, and the recognition from the public drove that idea, but I am telling you, my best move ever! I don't care anymore about the people, I simply loved them, and I think they are the most potent and meaningful tattoos around.

I will have to go back to finish it. I'm broke, so it will need to be after my book is out. I still missing the ying-yang logo, a climbing helmet and carabiner, a sit-ski, fins, mask and scuba tank. I don't really talk about them. I don't like talking about the uncertain future when there is no fact yet backing the idea. I prefer not talking about my future actions, and I speak rather about my accomplishments.

No Rest for the Wicked! Aka Kung Fu

I think I've done kung fu for about seven years. I started when I was in my first group home. I never anticipated being at that level at the beginning and doing it with both hemispheres of my body. I'm level V out of X. Basically, a belt level for kung fu compared to color in karate. The studio is very near my place but has not been all the time that case. When I was in Saddletowne, the studio was at two hours' bus ride most of the time, even more on a few occasions. During those long bus rides, I listened to my audiobooks. I did not care if it was longer; I was equipped for a long time. Most people would have quit, but not me, kung fu was already part of my life in the early days, existential in the last two years.

About for two years, I'm doing kung fu with my complete body. I suck really good, but I'm determined to be better one day. Let say that I stalled at level V and I will probably stay at that level for the rest of my life. I go twice a week at the studio. Usually on Wednesday I run solo when the other students are in the class. Solo because I need to review on my own because kung fu is the activity where I'm super dumb. I'm not joking, using my brain like two separate minds, one part needs to control the left, and I really need to focus on moving the right side. After the class, my private lesson goes on for about forty-five minutes with Dai Sihing. In private, I'm working extra hard only on my right arm. After forty-five minutes, I'm exhausted, not physically, but mentally. Usually, I survive because I'm not with the group before.

Friday is my big day of kung fu. I begin with the class. By the way, I attend a regular class with able-bodied people. Dai Sihing is the class instructor. That is the name of the guy number two, but in reality, that it is his kung fu name. Sifus is the big boss. I do most techniques with my right side. I kicked too, but my kick is pretty weak. Afterwards, I put on my climbing helmet, transfer belt and go for a walk with my walker. Dai Sihing and another student assist my eighty-meters walk. No rest for the wicked, I go right after into my private lesson. I try to last the complete forty-five minutes like on Wednesday, but I usually go until I reach complete exhaustion. Back home in the afternoon, I'm so dead that I take a three hours' nap.

When I'm not at kung fu, I have my brace on my right wrist and torque my arm to be able to open my hand palm up. I discovered my muscle relaxant by trying out the DR. HO TENS machine. It was so effective that the days of expensive BOTOX was over. I went from $12, 000 to zero dollars in a few months. I TENS my right arm every day, in my bed, before going to sleep. The last time I had BOTOX was two years ago. My arm is not at all spastic and my range of motion is almost the same as the left side.

I believe that methylphenidate has the same effect on everybody, including me. I consider myself smart before, but it was still under control. I notice that I was brilliant when I started to do kung fu with my entire body, which is two years ago, at the same time that I flushed the BOTOX. Before, doctors gave me a pill for every reason. I had about twenty capsules a day. Now, I'm smart about my health, and I'm down to one kind, six times a day. That pill is for the "Parkinson" type of movement in my complete body. All the other ones were totally useless.

Just a Pastime!

Once a week, I attend the adult program at Indefinite Arts. I go Wednesday morning at kung fu, and I go from there at around noon to Indefinite Arts. I get there about thirty minutes before the program, and I used this time to have my lunch. I mostly spend my time these days in the ceramic/pottery area, but I used the complete facility quite frequently. I've been going since 2011.

In the first couple of years, I was only good at leatherwork. Then, slowly, I started to open my horizon but was still doing leatherwork quite frequently. Then I moved from the group home to live by myself. I imagined a piece of art like I never made before. I started to make Yellow Edge. I went from making wallets to this incredible piece. I think it is the best of my best. Every art piece has something magical. I know, I'm way better now, but there is something to the basicness and the creativity of Yellow Edge. I did not even think hard; it is as if I knew what I was doing, like if I made a plan years ago and happened to rediscover or found again some old idea. It was with me all those years, I forgot but now the moment of execution has come.

I guess people usually get better with time! I think I'm different. I have another example that it was not a fluke. Again, it was nothing I expected to do, I was just doing experimentation and that mostly to kill time. I decided that I would take a shot at painting. Not knowing what I was doing,

First realistic painting and second one all together Photo Remy Bernier

I did *Rundle*. Not too shabby!

It seems the more I get to experience and try hard, the more sophisticated the project is and it is never as good as the first time. I did a few pieces with nothing expected in return, and maybe they are my best, simpler and more meaningful.

I believe I will master the technique quite fast, and those more complicated pieces will be my best one day. I'm still quite green, but I'm learning very fast. I think that I am a couple of years in advance of the program. I did not expect that at all, but what can I say: I will take it!

Art was simply a way to kill time. My artistic mind will maybe come to my rescue because nobody can deny my art. And remember, this is coming from someone who cannot even sign his name. On this note, just because I cannot sign but still want to do art at a high level, I came up with the idea of leaving the top edge of the canvas unfinished. Nobody is doing that nor will they, so I created my trademark. By leaving the top side unfinished, I can authentic my works of art in a way that is more powerful than just a signature. Being the top edge, nobody will see that it is unfinished.

Swimming like a Rock!

Every week I go all the way to YMCA Saddletowne. It's out of the way, but I believe it is the only pool equipped with a ramp in Calgary, and anyway, it is so far away that I get a direct ride with Access nine of ten times. I used to ride every time on the regular transit, but now, I feel lazy, and I enjoyed the convenience of Access Calgary. That is the only sign of ageing I could find over the years with me. I've been going there every week for six years, from the time back at the group home in Saddletowne. Everybody knows me by my name, I don't remember most of their names, but I know well faces. I feel as if I'm going to visit my family every time. I love it mostly because it is full of twentyish-year-olds. I get very along with that age group. The more they get older, the less I have that magic connection. It will be funny if I still get together well with that age group when I am sixty-plus years old. A little word about that I go only solo because I like to be so independent. Not because I don't have any helpers but because I want to be free.

I have swum every week for about nine years. With a worker at first and I hated that with a passion. It took me a few years to get my system dialed. When I moved to Saddletowne, my system was a theory first, but came the norm very quickly, and I did not modify any step for six and counting years. I broke it down to less than five minutes, for every time the lifeguard needs to handle me.

To get in the water wheelchair, I stand up at the transfer bar in the family changing room. Once I'm up, the lifeguard switches my chair for the water wheelchair. I lower myself in the water wheelchair and, just in a blink of an eye, I'm good to go. In the pool area, he puts on me some fins and a life jacket. To lower me in the water, he grabs one side of the wheelchair. With my help to keep it straight, he pushes the chair from the side of the ramp. That way, he doesn't get wet, putting me in the pool.

I swim for one hour on my back, kicking with the fins to propel me. Being so long in the water it is almost impossible not to freeze. That is why I wear the top of wetsuit with full zip, one on the large side so I can take it off quickly. It is way too big, but I don't care because I always have a life jacket on top, so actually it doesn't feel too big in the water. Make note that all my clothes are large because I don't want to fight in getting into medium-sized clothes. In that case, a medium-sized wetsuit would be perfect, but then, it would make the experience so much complicated for the lifeguard.

After one hour, everything is done in reverse to get me out of the water. After dropping the fins and removing my wetsuit, I go in the hot tub for fifteen-to-twenty minutes. I lose everything except my life jacket, and I load things back up in precisely the same way.

To get back in my wheelchair, he needs to reverse the same step except, this time, he puts a plastic bag and a towel on my seat. When he is gone, I bridge and unload my cushion to remove my swimsuit. I have to remove the towel and plastic bag, and I'm back to where I was before the adventure. I believe that the system is so straightforward and dumb proof that I don't know why more don't people use it!

Right, I'm the only one who can come up with that stuff. Anyway, I hope many will use it. Maybe it will be a few struggles at first, but such a freedom release when it is dialed. With all the activities I do, swimming is by far my favorite one. The peak of every week is me going to the pool. I think it is where I shine, and I act as really myself. The Genesis Center is my second home. I usually book three hours, so I'm not stressed by the time I finish. I use the extra time before my bus to have my lunch. It is also where I see my doctor in the clinic downstairs. I saw my doctor almost every month, and I would probably never figure out what it is going on with me if his office was external to the Genesis Center.

Big Boy Live Along!

Yes, I have many disabilities, and I am very proud to say that I live alone. My doctor suggested I should go to a group home to make new friends, and my answer was right away; NO WAY! I live in a deluxe apartment (deluxe to my standard, pretty normal otherwise). I have two bedrooms (one for all my junk), an open kitchen and with a lot of room as well as a built-in kitchen counter that it is a dining table at the same time. It has all the appliances, including stove and dishwasher, I can spin around in the bathroom with my power wheelchair and it is equipped with a walk-in shower. A balcony and open living room complete the tour. At only two blocks of Chinook Center, it lies seven minutes from the C-train in a highly concentrated business area, perfect for all my needs from Home Depot, Staple, Mark's Warehouse, a bank, drugstore and all the shops including in the biggest Mall in Calgary. Anyway, this comes out of my budget at $1100 a month but CUPS is helping me out to pay. CUPS is a non-profit organization that "Builds resilient lives for Calgarians facing the challenges of poverty and trauma." I pay $555 and they take care of the rest.

I feel like a king! I love my apartment so much. The only disadvantage is the snow removal during the winter. When it snows, I'm bound to my apartment, or I'm limited to run a circle around the block because it is impossible to cross the street without getting stuck. Anyway, I will take, anytime, a few months a year of snow for all the advantages the rest of the year.

At home, I barely need help every couple of months. I don't do any of the fun stuff which is cleaning, laundry, cooking and washing dishes. I have all that free time to work on my computer. You're probably thinking *How can he find the time?* Easy, I have a lot of time eliminating all the household works. I don't like watching television, and I listen to music all the time. I spent most of my days writing. Compared to the pace of my first book, I'm on fire for this one. I guess that is what methylphenidate can do for you.

I spend all day thinking, as well. I'm a thinking machine, even if I stopped the methylphenidate. The first time I stopped, I was listening to nature music and paused my audiobook. This time around, the difference is that I stopped gradually, and I'm still listening to my music and audiobooks. I'm actually smarter than before, and my eye is better every day. It is as if all the sleep I have is actually making me smarter. I'm not so much stuck on idea super weird, so weird that it is stupid to think like this. Before, I tried to reinvent the wheel when it was unnecessary.

I get a cleaner twice a month, every two weeks that keeps my apartment in check and does my laundry. Three hours my cleaner beats any way you look at it, ten hours of homecare. I was tire of them doing a lousy job. For example, they are so lazy that they don't take the time to wipe under an object on the counter; they do a shitty job contouring whatever is on the table. I have very low patience with lazy people. I may drop Homecare, but I get a way better service and super cheap, too. I almost have no dishes because I use Meals on Wheels. My special lunch doesn't need plates. You will know about it in the next section.

Because I qualify for two visits a week with Home Care, I needed to figure a way to have a shower every day. If I don't have my shower every day, my right foot freezes otherwise. I have thirty-eight pairs of socks at $25 each. I'm not kidding at all; I need to baby it a lot. I have neural pain that is mysterious for every doctor. Of course, they gave me a pill that does not affect my foot at all. I discontinued every single medicine for my weird problem that does not work. I used to be a drug junky with twenty tablets a day. Now I use Dantrium, two tablets three times a day. That is it! My blisters pack used to be quite impressive with all those pills. Now, it's looking somewhat empty.

Same Habit, Different Approach!

No more Bookshare for now. I will return for sure using the service for my favorite mountaineering books. I'm borrowing a real audiobook from the library. I know what was bugging me so much about the library. There are so, so many books available, and there are only a few that are up to my standard. I tried really hard to listen to new books, but they were all boring after fifteen minutes, to the point that I quit listening to them. So, I'm still stubborn enough to hear the same books over and over, but now my selection varies. I think I need a good break from mountaineering books. I've been listening to those same ten books for at least six years. I went back to my classics.

My first on my list was *The Big Tinny*. Maybe it was, I simply to be reminded how to live life without being too much consumed by the frame, the society set. Basically it shows how to be happy in a house no more significant than the space of a room. I loved this book. I've listened to it now three times. It was so long ago last time that it was as if I'd read a new book. It was all very different to my mountaineering books, but just as good. I know I'm very picky, but when I come across a good book like this one, I make sure to relisten to it once in a while.

My second was *Ice* (Ice-T). I will say that it is the best audiobook of all. Maybe it's not the cup of tea of everyone, but I simply love that shit. It is incredibly entertaining at literally every word. The coarse language, the gangster lifestyle, the street background, the rapper underground, etc…, made that book very unique. Maybe I loved that book so much because I don't give a shit about what people are saying behind my back. I read it four times, and I will be sure not to wait that long between readings. I tell you, it is the most entertaining book made of all time.

On my list, *The Secret Race, Inside the Hidden World of the Tour de France, Heavier Than Heaven* (a biography of Kurt Cobain) and *Open* (a biography of Andre Agassi). I did not listen to those books yet, but I had read those couple of times a long time ago. Another library issue is that I'm restricted from borrowing those books when my turn is up. Since they are more popular books, the wait might be a while. That what I love with Bookshare; there is no waiting. If you want a book and they have it, you can download it instantly. The downside of this, they are read by a computer-generated voice. My list is so good that I'm not looking at the reading experience but the book itself.

Another bad or good habit is from television. I can't stand watching it at all other than my shows of *Gold Rush*, *Homestead Rescue* and *Expedition Unknown*. There also is one show that I love on Netflix: *Suit*. Again, I tried hard to listen to new shows, but it just doesn't click. I'm watching the series for the third time. Being a very long show, I take many, many months to go through it all. I started the set five months ago, and I still have three seasons to go. I'm getting to be an expert in the subject and the way around the law. For sure, I'm not impressed by real lawyers. I know that I have a case against Alberta Health Services. Even if I do a trial on my hospital psychiatric experience only, I believe it will be an easy win, to prove that I'm a victim of the worst case of discrimination. I have only to get my books as a piece of evidence. But in reality, they did way more permanent damage to my health by prescribing me methylphenidate. The list is quite long. I contacted about twenty-five lawyers from Calgary and Edmonton, but I got a response from only five. And they were not interested in taking my case — so much energy spent on absolutely nothing. My little finger is telling me that they only not responded to me because I have a set of wheels. Just out of respect, they should all react even to say to me that they don't want the case. No way would I have such a low response if I was able-bodied.

Hell Gate!

Reviewing my book, I notice I was missing maybe the most important part: my stay at the hospital. For me, this represents my true hell gate. I usually forget people quickly, even if they are discriminating against me — everybody except my hospital stay.

I was clear enough to say what my problem was. I could not sleep but had to be resting for seven hours every night. You're wondering why I'm unsecured with people who don't know me (described in the first book)? Well, I think you have your answer with my stay at the hospital.

I said I should go to Unit 58 (a rehabilitation unit of the Foothills). Doctors should know what they are doing. I did not want to tell them how to do their job. One red flag is I stopped all my pill the day before my admittance. I like to say for my defense; I finished the Dantrium only for one day. After the first day, I saw the advantages of taking that pill. Still this day, I'm taking only the Dantrium. I told my Metaphenidate story, but nobody took me seriously. I saw a psychologist, and she asked me a bunch of questions related to superheroes and shit like that. A warning sign should come on, but when I'm fixing on something, I don't see what is around. I was going to Unit 58 to make sure of my mind.

The doctor told me I was going to the psychiatric unit. He told me if I want the problem fixed, that is the place to go. I'm maybe smart, but I'm also ignorant. I did not know what 'psychiatric' means.

Right from the start, everything was wrong. No bathroom where my wheelchair fits, no sink for brushing my teeth, etc… Nobody even knew how to transfer and basically, all the staff didn't realize my unique needs. I survived because I'm extra stubborn to be as healthy as I could be. If it were someone else, the staff would end up with a severe problem. Do you think it is normal for a guy who cannot even stand up one second to be functional in an environment for an able-bodied person?

I finally found a bathroom in the High operation for the real trouble mind. To not end up on the floor, I rode the toilet backward — feet along the wall and back toward the front. I used to do the transfer on my own three to four times a day. Not that I needed to go for a number two every time but to deliver me from my agony. After five days, I stayed in bed all afternoon because I was starting to have bedsores. I rang the call bell four times, paged Doctor Nuts twice and once the ER doctor. Nobody gave a shit! I started to be really, really mad inside. From that time on, I had only one answer to their question: no comments!

I was so pissed off, but nobody realized it or noticed it. I guess I'm good at hiding my emotions. I was also pissed off because they didn't do anything yet to help me sleep. I took charge of the situation on day number one. I requested a shower every night and a freshly made bed every day. The shower was kind of funny to see the nurse, clueless. It was okay only because I told them, about fifty steps they need to do. If they had any other patient, they would have serious issues. I needed a mechanical lift, but of course, they had none.

I stayed so long because I refused to take a mood-stabilizer pill. I knew I was far from manic, even if the doctors told me so many times that I was manic. Almost every day, they asked me about my mood, and it was always a ten. Why did they ask me that question if, no matter the answer, they would recommend taking the pill? One major part of been manic is to be violent to some degree. I never show a sign of physical or verbal threat to even my worst enemy. They did tag me the same as murder? Where is that coming from?

I knew I faced the most extreme case of discrimination. The story does not end there, but three months later, after $2,500 of cushions and everybody, including my love, thinking I'm missing a few screws and avoiding talking to me. My first round with the media didn't go as plan. I told my doctor, I'm willing to drop the charge if AHS undo their big mess; I'm a victim here, and almost everybody doesn't want to talk to me, scared I will start talking crazy shit, I guess?

I went to see my doctor determined to get AHS to clean up their mess, but he told me that he couldn't help me. He referred me to a social worker. I don't know what a social worker will do differently? Anyway, I contacted five agencies that offer to advocate. I'm determined to get what I want, without any useless help from AHS. If I don't get an advocate, I will send my letter alone. I gave AHS the chance to redeem themselves, but they did absolutely nothing.

Note: I emailed five agencies that offer advocacy, and none responded. I must stink or what? I'm scaring everybody away with my stories. How good those agencies are if somebody, like me, needs serious help and they don't take the time to respond? I tell you, there is a severe glitch in society!

Freaking Methylphenidate!

I'm pissed off by the fact that I'm smarter doesn't make up for all the grief that happens to me over the years. I'm already very disabled; I did not need that problem on top. Everything seems to be falling into place since I stopped. The eye specialist told me I have nystagmus. I don't have nystagmus at all; my problem was a side effect of the methylphenidate. Almost two months from the time I stopped and my vision is better day after day. Now, it is just shaky a few minutes a couple of times a day. It was shaky at my computer during the first month, and now, it is gone altogether! It was acting up for two hours in the morning, and one hour at night; now, I don't have any more downtime. My eyesight goes three times further. I bet, in one year, it will be as healthy as anyone's.

My right foot was affected by a strange sweating problem. I end up at the Emergency, and they had nothing more for me than giving me a nasty pill. Me trusting the doctors, I did nothing less than listen to them because of they're a kind of god to me. Now that I stopped the methylphenidate, my foot is not sweating and creates its own heat. I wear my shoes all day; I don't need to change my socks five times, don't need booties any more, I don't need three-dozen pairs of socks at $25 each and don't need to put my winter boots on when it is above freezing. For two years, everything was a plan around my foot; it was so severe that I ended up at the hospital. For the first time in ten months, I don't care about taking a shower every night. I can go sleeping over and not worry about my foot. I didn't go anywhere in the last months, where it was impossible to take the mandatory showers.

During the nights, I never, never, sweat any more. When I'm warm, I don't sweat; I'm just feeling hot. It was getting ridiculous trying to find a way to regulate the temperature. Now, I don't even care if it is a little bit too warm. Before, I was stressed every night that the temperature was to get too warm. And the temperature never got warm, I'm the one whose internal thermometer was fucked up. I was trying to cool down my apartment to the point it was freezing in the morning. I went as far as opening the window in the middle of the winter. Besides my foot, my sleeping habits kept me now from sleeping out.

I said that because of the gabapentin, my sperm was bright fluorescent yellow. Sorry, I made a mistake. It was still bright yellow because it was not long enough after I stopped the methylphenidate. Now, after two months, the color is changing from yellow to white. I don't want to take any chance, no babies from me. He will probably have two heads or be super handicapped.

Those are only four critical things that bugged me that were fixed by discontinuing the methylphenidate. I tell you, if I had the choice between being smart or all those problems being fixed, I'd take without any hesitation no problem over being smart. Anyway, being smart is another problem as nobody has recognized it. So far, I had no good from it! At least without the chemical, I would live life to the fullest and not been so bored that…

12-01-19

I'm not very happy! It's been six months since I took last my final dose of methylphenidate. Everything is falling into place. Turn out; I took close to twenty pills for many weird problems when it was the methylphenidate that was guilty from the beginning. I really understand what is going on, and this is what happened from the start, no doubt about it.

The first time I was admitted at the Emergency was for a strange reaction between the methylphenidate and the pill I was taking for curing my lactose and gluten intolerance. Every time I had food with a high level of acidity, I was becoming lactose and gluten intolerant. No doctors heard about this because it is a pure fact of my imagination (sarcastic). I was so sick; I could not have a slight trace of gluten or lactose. I had three crises that I cured with a general antibiotic. The doctors were skeptical that I fixed my problem with that antibiotic. One refused to give me the medicine until I made a total scene, he gave me some just to keep me under control and to shut me up. The third time, it was way more severe. In fact, I was experiencing a significant high. I had considerable vertigo and was seeing the world spinning. Doctors tried to find what it was wrong with me, couldn't figure it out, so they assumed I was faking. They took me by force, in the waiting area. I fell asleep in the process. I was awakened by the cops, covered in my pee. I peed in my pants while I was sleeping. The police were there to arrest me. They had no way to transport my wheelchair, so they called a cab to bring me home. I woke up ten hours later, and everything was back to normal, including my lactose and gluten intolerance. Everybody thought I was a liar, including my caseload manager at the group home. I was evicted two months later because they couldn't trust me anymore, and other made-up bullshit.

The second time I was admitted was for my foot. Today, my foot is as healthy as the other one. I even put my shoes in -15. Before, I was putting my winter boots (ratted -30) at +5. The last time I felt like this was before my stroke. One significant side effect of methylphenidate is the constriction of blood vessels of the extremities. No shit. It was way beyond a little circulation problem. It felt like no blood at all was going to my foot. I had the TENS machine on non-stop for a year. That was the only reason why I didn't go sooner to the hospital. The TENS kept pumping blood to my foot. The doctors gave me more pills instead of looking more deeply into the problem.

We all know about my last visit. I like to point out that, here again, the guilty party is the methylphenidate. I'm not inventing those side-effects; they are all taken from the web page: https://www.webmd.com/drugs/2/drug-9475/ritalin-oral/details/list-sideeffects?fbclid=IwAR2jWhf-NAHgIV1F9ZcHL9rdag26nyVsiViPASqvpVC_WNJr1NS7f_GbCsE. Those four are the ones that affected me: Manic Behavior, Difficulty Sleeping, Excessive Sweating and Over Excitement. Again, nobody tried to see the big picture. I knew by then that it was because of the methylphenidate. I expressed my concern and instead of taking me seriously, they locked me down with the tag of murder.

Those problems are only the ones that I went to the hospital. After three chances, they should cut it out, and if somebody had listened to me seriously on the third visit, all that bullshit could be straightened out. By the end, I said clearly what was wrong with me, so the only reason I was put in the psychiatric unit was by pure discrimination from the hospital staff.

Those are only the reasons I got hospitalized. There is still the stuff that was bogging my mind at the beginning of this chapter. And there is also the stuff I did not know, like weight loss, a fast heartbeat and chronic muscle twitches or movements. There is also my problem like gastric acid that is not recorded as a possible side effect, but is most likely related.

01/11/20

Another reason to mad of the pill and one of the most severe impacts on my health comes in the next chapter. I will not ruin the suspense of the book. Say that I know mostly the effect of the pill, but the list keeps growing with time. I probably never will know all the wrong stuff it did to me.

Part 2:
Think Outside the box!

Diet: Think outside the box!

Want to know about weight management for a power wheelchair user and people who want to lose weight?

It's about time someone writes on weight management for someone in a power wheelchair and proposes a diet that works. I haven't had any extra fat for five years.

First of all, when I moved out of the group home to live on my own, I needed to lose all that extra weight, which was about forty pounds. I lost forty-three pounds in the first two months. Interested in how this happened?

I moved to the Mustard Seed, a low-income facility with mostly people who come from a homeless background and with disabilities. They gave us super-active vitamins; it did not matter what you ate to be healthy. I'm not at the Mustard Seed any more, but I buy precisely the same vitamins. For five years, I had nothing more than juice, Cliff bar and dry mango for lunch. I kept my weight of 143 pounds with no fluctuation for five years. I had a typical breakfast and a frozen meal from Meals On Wheels for dinner.

Here is the reality for a wheelchair user:

We need about 900 calories to have a steady weight. Why are there only a few slim people in a a power wheelchair? If they live in a group home or institute, their diet is based on 2, 000 calories, which is what an able-bodied person needs.

I had many caregivers in the seven years I was in a group

home. I can tell you right away; they are unaware of the unique needs of someone in a wheelchair when it comes to food. They have a bunch of training, but few understand the importance of diet. They cook according to their knowledge, which is cooking on an intake of 2, 000 calories. Also, they pity us, so they give us a super portion thinking that will be good for us. So if you are in a group home, you are most likely getting fat like I was.

The only population that seems to have escaped this reality are the ones who are tube fed. I have never seen a fat tube-fed person. What do they eat? A super healthy formula call Ensure. As far I know, they seem pretty healthy. I was tube fed for two months, and I never lacked nutrition or felt undernourished. It must be good stuff if they give you that at the hospital.

I was so broke at one time that I decided for two months try my theory. Indeed, I did not have real food for two months. I felt wonderful. I did not experience any loss of energy. I stopped after two months because I'm not stupid enough to jeopardize my health based on a theory without scientific facts.

Around the same time, the pill ranitidine went under recall, so I decided to stop taking antacid pills since I'm barely taking any pills (I was on it for six years). Then I started to experience bad gastric acid reflux. I thought that my diet was terrible, so I stopped after two months. With real food, the acid was insane, so I contacted my doctor to give me a new pill. I tried the new tablet once, and I reacted badly to the medicine. I requested another pill, and finally, I had a breakthrough.

I was taking twelve billion probiotics for five years. The

combination of the ranitidine and probiotic seems to do the trick, but the probiotic alone was way under what I needed. After a week on the pill recommended by my doctor, I ventured to the drug store, and got myself two months of insane probiotics sixty billion cells. It turned out I don't need the useless pill recommended by my doctor. I need simply to take potent probiotics every day because the methylphenidate killed most of the enzymes in my stomach, so there's another reason to be pissed off at that pill.

Everybody that I spoke about my diet categorized me as crazy. Even if I believed in the theory, I stopped because I'm tired of people thinking that I'm insane when I'm really not. I just see the world from another perspective, but other than this, I'm not any different than you.

I personally consider cooking, washing dishes and going to the grocery store a waste of time. What may take two minutes for an able-bodied person could take me half hour. I have many challenges with my handicap; by living alone, I took some of the challenges away.

By societal standards, it is not normal to have so many severe disabilities and live alone. That said, I would never trade places with anyone, including able-bodied people. I don't have to work, cook, go grocery shopping, clean or do laundry (cleaners do all that fun stuff). I have all that spare time to play and enjoy life. And who said healthy is more expensive? I lost count, and I don't want to figure it, but I save somewhere between a quarter and half and more than 75% on Ensure.

The diet is super simple, and I bet it is the healthiest.

I approach two dietitians to write something, but they were speechless. I bet it's because I completely destroyed their beliefs and profession. By the way, I'm not here to judge what is legit and what is not; I will leave that to you to draw your own conclusions.

First off: be ready to take a lot of capsules in the morning. I'm used to it because I use to take twenty pills a day, now only one type. Why? I don't know; maybe I'm healthier? You need to take the following every day. Two of Multi, two of 1, 000 milligrams of vitamin C, one of 1, 000 milligrams of Omega 3, one of 100 micrograms of K2, one of 500 milligrams of magnesium, one of six to twelve billion cells of probiotic, one of 1, 000 micrograms of B12, seven drops of D3 and one of 650 milligrams of calcium. If you take all those essential vitamins, now you can eat whatever you want to be healthy. Try to figure out what works for you.

Having my meals for dinner delivered, I never need to go to the grocery store more than once every couple of months.

To give you an example, I will describe my diet:
Breakfast
Two waffles with syrup
Green tea
Five tubs of trail mix
Lunch
600 milliliters of flavored water (water with few drops of lime juice)
Cliff bar
Five to eight pieces of low sugar dry mango

Dinner
Frozen meal from Meals on Wheels
500 to 750 milliliters of flavored water

Snack
Up to half a cup of chia chips

That diet is working for me. I even put on some weight, but I don't care as long I'm below 155 pounds. All my mango, trail mix and chia chips are coming from www.nuts.com. I buy in large quantities, so I get food for six months to one year. I get my Cliff bars delivered to me for free at www.walmart.ca. I need to go to the grocery store every three months or so to get waffles.

A couple of years ago, I was walloped by a sickness. I suffered three days of fever, and I had a hard time breathing. By day four, I was full of energy and my illness was behind me. I started to expel a massive amount of green mucus from my lungs. By and large, this was a mean average of one to 1.5 liters. I recovered from a significant lung infection in three days without a doctor or drugs. People die from this stuff! But I walked away after three days.

I visited Jacynthe when she had a very nasty sinus infection. I think she struggled for one month. Of course, I caught the virus. I was down for one day with a fever and the next day, I felt like nothing had happened.

Recently, I woke up with a terrible eye infection three times. I could barely open my eye, it was watery, and my nose was plugged. By lunch, it was way better but not completely healed. The following day, it was like nothing had happened at all.

My prescription glasses are pretty much the same since I started taking my vitamins five years ago. And I use my eyes much more these days, with my books and continuous writing. In the period before the vitamins, I was changing glasses like everybody else without putting my eye to the real stress of writing. Sometimes, the page is all out of focus that I can't see my eighteen-size print, but I keep going at it, and my vision does not suffer.

Last time I had a cold that lasted more than one day it was probably more than five years ago. I tell you, this is not a joke. Every sickness lasted one day except for my bad lung infection that lasted three days.

I'm not any different to you. If you want to judge me and you are not convinced of my story, I say to you: do your research and leave me alone.

The hospitals are filled with sick patients that do not need medical attention. If more people were doing what I'm doing, hospitals and doctors' offices would be almost vacant. You can go with my diet or be hospitalized for every small bug. It doesn't matter because I made my choice. I'd rather stay as far as possible from the hospital. The only good thing they did to me is saving my life with my stroke, everything else was bullshit.

If it were not for my vitamins, I would probably be very sick mentally, or even worse, be dead. I'm a victim of a significant medical fuck-up, and I consider myself very lucky that I caught it without much grief. There is only one thing that is a mystery; how have I become so smart? It does not bother me; in fact, I don't care as long people give me what I deserve.

Every single person told me that what I was doing wasn't right for my health. That if I want to be healthy, I'm better having my vitamins with food than with tablets. Easy to say but totally impossible for me. Keep in mind that I have no money even to buy milk. I'm buying my vitamins only this year. The four years prior, they were totally free for someone poor like me, with supplies from Pure North. With my vitamins, I was so healthy that I dodged a real mental illness at best, death at worse.

I get judged for every action I take. Instead of looking at what others do, it's better stay focus on yourself and let others live their lives the way they want. Anyway, I believe everyone is doing their best with their life (most people anyway).

I had a psychologist therapist that I went to only once because, obviously, he would try to change me for the worse. I have high hopes with this book that people will understand and give me a break.

Cell Phone Always Ready to Go!

Don't miss a call ever again. In my case, I used to miss almost every single one. I needed to come up with a solution, and after trying many things, I came up with the ultimate solution.

This trick only works if you use a wheelchair and the belt. Now, I eliminated the need for a watch because my phone is always on my lap and I can see the time. I can use all features of the phone from this handy location. If I want to listen to an audiobook, my earbuds are still easy to access on the side of my wheelchair. Since it is on a leash, I don't need to worry about losing my phone or someone stealing it. I've been doing this trick for about eight years and have never had an issue. It is the ultimate technique for effective phone management.

You can buy everything you need for less than seven dollars (phone case not included). If you get a clear phone case, you will be able to display your bus pass by inserting it between the phone and the phone's case. Taking the transit is made an easy, fast and super-efficient way to show your pass. It sits on your lap all the time.

Make two holes about three millimeters to attach the rope. You can drill or melt the punctures in the case. If you decide to go with melting, take a nail and warm it with a lighter until it is warm enough to melt the holes. In some applications, it is not possible to use the melting technique, so use the drill if that is the case.

Use about thirty centimeters of two-millimeter rope from a shop that specializes in outdoor apparel. Make it shorter if you don't need to deal with colder temperatures. I have it on a longer leash because I tuck the phone away from the elements under my winter jacket. The cold temperature eats up the battery so this helps to avoid the unit from freezing up.

Buy the cheapest but real carabiner at the same outdoor shop you got the rope. Use an overhand knot to complete the loop with half an inch of tail. Use the carabiner to complete the link to your belt. The phone is now secured, with quality parts that will never break.

A couple of years ago I used the factory leash that came with my phone case. The first time I used it, my phone went missing. The only reason I got my phone back is because the headphones were still attached to it. Since that day, I trust only my rig. Then I don't have to worry, because I know that my phone is always secure on my belt.

Now, the physical modification is done, let's complete the job with the setting of the phone. Not every phone has great accessibility features. I use Apple iPhone for its features. I pick that phone first for its low vision feature, but now, the "answering" feature is the handiest.

Go into settings on your phone. Select "Call Audio Routing" to speaker and select Auto-Answer Calls. Now, if the phone is ringing, you have absolutely nothing left to do. To be even more efficient (and courteous to those around you) use earbuds with a microphone when you are out. Don't forget to select "Call Audio Routing" to Automatic.

If your phone doesn't have these features, you will need to answer the call and then put it on speakerphone.

Depending on your level of ability, you may or may not want to add a phone holder. For me, it is a vital feature to keep a firm grip on the phone; otherwise, I'd drop it.

01/11/2020

That cellphone trick is fantastic for when you go out but is inconvenient around the house if you dislike talking true handsfree. In this case, you need a new trick for answering the phone when you're at home.

The answer is simple: just add Velcro! Velcro that is on industrial-strength tape. It is very handy. I use it all the time for everything and bought three meters ten years ago. I still have some, but I will need to get more for the next project.

Cut a small piece of the smooth part (about 2 cm x 2 cm).

Stick it to your phone beside the camera.

Cut a bigger piece on the rough half (about 3 cm x 3 cm).

With the tape still on the back, Velcro with the part on the phone so the small piece is in the middle of the bigger piece.

Take the tape off and stick it wherever you want on your wheelchair.

Note: you may need to cut larger pieces if you decide to stick it under your seat. I used a smaller bit because the weight of the phone is resting in a small pocket on my kangaroo bag attach to my seat.

At night, I have a rough Velcro stick to my transfer pole, so I stick the phone to it.

Fitted Sheet in Bed

For someone like me, it is impossible to keep a bedsheet organized under blankets.

For the longest time, I used a duvet, but I've found that this is not for me.

My choices were pretty limited, as I prefer a heavy cover without any insulation (synthetic or duvet). I got myself a vintage Quebec traditional catalogne and quilt. Now, the tricky part was to keep the sheet underneath organized. But I had the solution way before I ordered the blankets.

For years, I kept a fitted sheet in my bed for the warm nights, which was almost every night. That trick works with any fitted sheet, but the one that isn't of elastic works best for taller persons. Personally, I use the one elastic tight, which is not ideal, but also it is impossible to get unstuck.

Simply wedge your body in the sheet and go under your covers. Put the elastic over your knees to release tension in the elastic. For someone who always has cold feet, this technique is ideal because it makes you feel as if your feet are in a sleeping bag. I tell you; this is the only way to keep a sheet organized. Even if you're someone who moves around a lot.

I've been using this trick for over six years now!

3/14/2020

I found a way, way better trick. My cleaner did not

understand my thing with my two fitted sheets. Anyway, he put the two layers on top of each other, around the mattress. I was pissed off at first when I realized, but then a bulb came up. I took out the top sheet from underneath the mattress on the head side and simply slid between the two fitted sheets, under the covers. It's impossible to get the upper layer off the end of the bed. I feel like it is exactly like my bed before my accident, no elastic bugging me. I'm a side sleeper, so it does not matter if the sheet is tight. To avoid having a tight sheet, just use one side tucked in (feet)! Originally, I thought that the sheet had to be installed first and then removed from head but this step is useless. I had, lately, my best sleep since my accident, which is thirteen years ago. I'm so excited that I'm looking for the time spent in bed. Weird, before I was looking forward to the long nights sleepless, and now I'm looking forward because I sleep so well.

Password Software

These days, you need a password for every Internet site. Filling out forms for buying items online is something that I avoid. With password software, all your passwords are managed with a simple click.

Using password software makes buying something or filling out a form less time-consuming. I have access to more than a hundred password sites. Buying something is just an easy click. Everybody should use a password manager, not just the disabled.

Text to Speech Software

Reading is nearly impossible with low vision. To read anything, I run the text in my Word to Speech software. I'm always current on stories over the web even if I cannot read them.

Word Prediction Software

Believe it or not, I wrote a 55,000-word book, typing only with one finger. It took me seven years, and I will publish it the next year! It usually takes me ten hours to complete a chapter that is 1, 000 words.

Word Prediction Software speeds things up by about five times the regular process. If I don't know how to write a word, I start to spell the word, and select it when it appears.

Grammarly

English is not my first language and I never went to school for it. I'm a terrible speller and grammar is not my cup of tea. I use Grammarly to give me a finish that I can be proud of. After I run Grammarly, I can't even recognize my text. It's that good!

The book you are reading now is a combination of the last three software packages that I use all the time for my bookmaking, film, reading, getting news, etc.

Laminated Floor on the Wall.

This trick is not mine, but it is so genius that I had to include it.

The trick is as simple as putting two rows of laminate floor on the walls. Use two screws per board. For a perfect look and to protect the corner, add a beautiful piece of trim in aluminum. You will need to glue the trim.

Now, even if you are clumsy like me, you will never make a ding in the wall with your wheelchair.

Nails

Living on my own, I needed to find a trick for trimming my nails. Most people in my situation would just go for a manicure every two weeks. I refuse to take the time and money for a problem so simple, so I put the thinking machine to work.

When I was flying on my own, I thought long and hard about this. Then I discovered a super-simple solution. The answer was right in front of me! The idea came to me as I was thinking about how birds use a sandpaper sleeve on the stand in their cages for filing down their beak and nails. A straightforward solution to something we do every day. Thanks to my new trick, I never have to deal with long nails any more.

After my bright idea, I went to the hardware store. Here is what you'll need to re-create my nail-filing solution:

400-grit sandpaper.
    One piece of plywood from the scrap wood of the store. (You could use from your own wood scrap if you have one.) Pick a longer board to put the clamp on to hold as an aid. Wide enough to cover the two faces of the board with one sheet of sandpaper.
    Glue the sandpaper to the plywood, use regular glue, stick style (school type).
    Put a rag underneath the board on top of the table or

countertop to avoid scratching the surface.

Clamp down the end with no sandpaper, and you grind your nails when you need it. I guarantee you won't have nails too long ever again.

Teatime!

I've heard a myth that warming water in the microwave is bad for you. Why is it wrong for water and okay with everything else?

My friend was pissed off because he could not find the kettle at a kayak camp. I told him, why should that matter if we have a microwave? His answer was he preferred to use a kettle for warming water. I didn't understand. Does water taste better in the kettle?

First of all, the top stove style is of the question for me. I don't want to burn down my building. The electrical one is better, but the cord is always in the way. Storage is not possible for me, so it's better to leave it on the counter for the morning anyway. And having limited counter space, I prefer to free up the area. I used an electric kettle a long time ago. While transferring the water to my mug, I spilled the content and burn myself pretty bad. That was the last time I used it.

Since that day, I warm up my water in a plastic cup with a line for the maximum level, no less and no extra. I put it in for a specific time in the microwave. The water is not boiling so it is way safer if I spill it.

In three years, I've never dropped it because the cup is so light and not bulky at all. After the hot water is transferred to my mug, I top it up with cold water to make my tea drinkable. I have my tea every morning, and my drink is always at the same temperature.

Part 3:
2020 is my Year!

Somebody Finally Recognizes my Work!

I spent New Year like everyone in the last decade, alone and in bed by nine thirty. I'm wondering if I will be luckier and if my book will be published in the New Year. I sent my manuscript to four publishers before Christmas, and I should get news in two to six weeks. I've become so used to getting bad news that I don't have faith in myself any more, but I still have some minuscule hope that somebody will pick up my book without costing me too much money. To me, it is clear; I deserve big time to have my book publish. I'm wondering if I am the only one who thinks this. Maybe it is because it is my book, but I really believe it is an incredible book and life story.

    Six months earlier, I sent my manuscript to two publishers oriented toward the outdoors and adventure. To me, it was clear from the beginning of the project that my book would be hosted by one of those two companies. It is only after they rejected me that I realized that my writing has only one part out of five on climbing. I was hit by a train. I never saw it coming; I was not prepared to face other options. Some time went by when I did nothing. Three months ago, I almost self-published an e-book. That is the only option I have that will not cost me too much money. I did not care about spending in the last year, but now my cards are killing me. I wished I would care more, but to me, I was sure that my book would be picked up. I did not plan the eventuality to self-publish; I could have a beautiful book self-publish if I would consider it. Publishing an e-book would put my book up there and with the chance to be picked up and printed in hard copy. It seems easy to self-publish an e-book but it's still a mountain to climb for someone like me. I think the step that discouraged me the most was the cover. Sure, I could figure it out, but it would be way less appealing than one made by professionals. An average cover would not reflect the high quality of my book. I gave up for the first time in the last decade to a challenge. Most likely because I'm not taking the methylphenidate any more. You see, I'm capable of failing, I'm also extremely drained of energy. I need to have some good happening to me because I'm about to give up. My dream and my labor of seven years looked as if it had come crashing down.

Another month passed by, and I did nothing. Then, my depressed mind found the motivation to keep the fight happening. I researched on the Web publishers that accept a manuscript for evaluation. I selected four. We are two weeks before Christmas, and I will hear back within two to six weeks in the new year. My batteries are filled instantly. I know, for sure, if they read my manuscript, they would do anything to get my book. There is nobody who will read my book. I started to believe it will be missed because nobody takes me seriously.

I had high hopes of hearing first from a prestigious publisher. Olympia was the first to the line. They offered me a contract that I could not refuse. I waited a week to hear from my main target. It turned out, they did not like my book, but I think it is the disturbing content they did not want to be associated with. Then, I was in total panic mode; I signed right away my contract with Olympia. I don't care if Olympia is not the most prominent publisher out there, but they are the only people who believed in me, including my family. Four weeks later, another publisher from the UK offered me a contract with precisely the same offer as Olympia. Knowing that another publisher believes in my work is telling me that I did not land Olympia by luck, but it was well deserved. My redemption has begun.

I am Looking for a Roommate!

It is Christmas, and I'm at Lee & Barb. They adopted two rescued cats. I told Barb that I want to have a cat, but I cannot afford it yet. I came back that night and realized how I would take a cat for my mental health right now. I always had big projects on the go, and my mind was never bored. Different in the last few months. Other than this book, I watched the time passing by, and I'm doing absolutely nothing constructive. The book is filling just a small part of the pie. I don't like watching TV other than *Suit* on Netflix. I decided that now is the time. I will find money because if I wait, I will be really a nutcase.

On the following day I sent emails to different rescue organizations (I had nothing else to do on Boxing Day). I wanted to go to the "rescue" way because I would not know the temper of the animal otherwise. I also needed the cat to be already trained with the litter. I mentioned in my email that I probably need an older cat who does not try to escape by the door every time I'm going out.

A few days later, I got a phone call from the Calgary Animal Rescue Society. They have the perfect kitten for me. They just received a surrender kitten with three legs. Hearing this, I fell automatically in love. He was so new that he wasn't ready to move until three weeks had passed. I was so eager to give the poor little thing a chance that I did not want to see him earlier because it would just inflame my excitement. He was six months old.

He finally moved in on Saturday, 18 January and the next Monday, I got the excellent news with Olympia. So far, the New Year is extraordinary! I'm sure, and only good will happen to me. Finally, after all those years of shit, I see the light at the end of the tunnel.

My new Best Friend!

Having a cat was my best move ever! I named him Cam, short for Camalot. I never feel bored any more. He is a tiny cat. He is only seven months old but, more than likely, he will remain small. He is just smaller than a usual cat. Being so little he is, to my eye, the cutest furball around. He loves me; he is asking almost all the time for attention. Being so cute, he gets a lot of my free time. He is all black except a patch of white on the belly and little bit of grey near the eyes and with yellow eyes.

I was told at first that he is born with three legs (two fronts and one back), later I was told they have no idea what happened to him. I sure know he is not born like that. In fact, I think it happened not too long ago. My best guess was three months ago. When I first got him a month ago, he did not let anyone near his missing leg. Now, one month later, he makes me pet his leg and touch his stump. When I first got him, his stump was in rough shape, with his bone somewhat still visible. Now the stump is really taking shape. Also, he still has the reflex of trying to scratch himself with the rear right leg, which is impossible because it is missing.

One back leg means he is not able to jump more than one to two feet. He is so perfect for me, he is always at ground level, and he doesn't try to escape. The first week, he did not leave me for twenty-four hours a day. He slept every night in my bed. To be sure I wasn't to ditch him, he slept right against me, with just the blankets between each other. After his litter break, he was back at the floor level, unable to get back in bed. The poor little thing was mewling at me like begged me, "Please, please, pick me up!" He was waking me up a few times a night. I really did not figure out that kitten until the second week, when I laid down my luggage on the ground at the end of the bed.

Now, he breaks the jump in two, so it is way more comfortable to manage than one super long leap. Going for the bed seems still quite the mission. He spends 75% of the night at the floor level. I guess it is asking too much to leap every night. I presume he spends the night in his favorite place, by the door, underneath my shoe rack. It is a little shelf about twenty-five centimeters off the ground. Against two walls, with shoes on top and one pair of shoes on the ground, it makes the ideal cave or hiding spot. When I told the lady at the rescue society how he doesn't like sleeping in the bed, she thought that it was kind of strange, like he did not like me. I said that he is a busy cat, and she laughed like she did not believe me.

Cam has a weird feeding pattern (I'm not the only one). Instead of eating a lot, a few times a day, he eats three to five palettes of dry food every one to two hours during the day and mostly during the night. He likes to play with his food. His plate is not restrained to his bowl but to all the kitchen floor. One by one he picks food pallets with his little paws and puts them on the floor. Then, sometimes he eats them, and sometimes, he sends the pallet spinning across the kitchen floor before eating it. During the night, I have no idea what he is doing before one o'clock because I sleep like a rock, but afterwards I hear him every hour playing with his food. Every morning, his bowl is almost empty. He eats no more than half a cup of dry food. Never, so far, have I come across cat food on the kitchen floor. Maybe, all the cats are the same, but if that is the case, we should take a few tricks from them. I think he is a genius; he entertains himself while eating about twenty times a day. When he sleeps with me, after three o'clock, I lose him because he needs to resume his eating habits.

The first two weeks, he was so skinny that the society told me to feed him twice a day with wet food. It took me a week to figure out how to open the food can. I bought fourteen cans of real tuna. He loves it, but the portion was way too big for him. I started to drain the leftover down the kitchen sink because my garbage bin was really stinky after one day with the leftover tuna. After two weeks, he was getting fat. I started to feed him the food the society gave me. He did not want a bite at the paté. That meal was the equivalent of fast food and hot dogs. I was throwing most of it in the LitterLocker (his garbage for his business). I started, at the same time, to feed him with the dry food recommended by the society. He preferred to starve than eat that junk. No wonder why he was so skinny from his foster home. The problem lasted only two days because I plugged the kitchen sink so severely that the wet food days were over. Since that day, he has only eaten dry food (different to the crap food from his foster home) and his weight is regular, now.

He likes to sleep on my lap, so I watch more TV than usual. I still think TV is boring. I watch only *Gold Rush*, *Homestead Rescue* and *Expedition Unknown*. When there is nothing good, I watch *Suit* on Netflix. Nowadays I find the show that

I loved, on the methylphenidate, *Mystery at the Museum*, so dull. It is too much of a slow pace for my liking.

I'm early up from my bed, between five thirty and six. Now I have something to do for one hour before my program. I use the spare time to play with Cam. But first thing when I wake up, I fill his water, food and clean his litter. I clean it every day, so it doesn't smell at all. I put his business in a LitterLock. When the bag is full, I ask the maintenance guy of my apartment building to replace it. He is a cat lover, and he is happy to help. My cleaner is not allowed to change Cam's litter box. Right from the first change, I scoop the dirty litter in a bag which is staying open in a box. Then my cleaner takes the bag to the garbage chute. Super easy, I don't know what people are doing, but this is the easiest and most clean way that I could come up with. People are saying I can't have a cat because I can't take care of the litter? Again, they are judging as if I can't do anything. Excuse me, but I cannot think of a more straightforward process. No matter what people think, they are all wrong again.

Maybe Crazy, Crazy Motivated!

For the two months before Christmas, I was doing nerve stimulation for up to three hours a day. My idol Tommy Caldwell did three hours of nerve stimulation for his cut finger. If Tommy did three, I would do three as well. He was using a jar full of macaroni, and I would use a pot full of rotini. I was putting and turning my right hand in the bowl while watching *Suit*. After three hours, my hand was really marked by the rotini. After a while, I got a bunch of tiny open wounds on my hand. I was also picking up loonies. I suck real bad at the last. When I found out Camalot was coming, I stopped like I had something else to look for and also because I found it useless. Was it useless? Three weeks after I stopped, I was doing my reinforcement exercises for my right arm at kung fu when, suddenly, my pinky finger was in terrible pain. It was the equivalent to a second-degree burn. It lasted for one hour after my kung fu session, and then it went away until dinnertime for two hours. I tell you, I'm super glad I stopped. All this wasn't to live in agony. That will teach me not to try to be superman.

All my life, I was good at sport but never gifted. In cross-country skiing, I was amongst the top athlete of my age in the country. I got to that point only by training, like a religion. Or more like a sect because, in my teens, I had no relationships outside my bubble of cross-country skiing.

What I consider the most impressive is my climbing.

Usually, only elite climbers go in the rock-guide course. I found myself amongst all those super-good climbers and I was just a recreation climber, with not even fifteen leads under my belt. A week before the course, I climbed and climbed. Basically, I needed to learn fast how to climb. The power of the mind is more potent than all the rest. I did well in the course, but I could only achieve this with my stubbornness to stick to the climbs. By the end, I was climbing above the requirement, but I was still barely climbing 5.12a (7a+). My niche seems to be 5.11d (7a), where I had many onsight. I was onsighting (on the first try) my top level of climbing except for a few redpoint (after many attempts) of 5.12a (7a+). After all the efforts I put in my climbing, I would be climbing at least 5.13 (7c+) if I was gifted (see Remy Bernier @ 8a.nu).

The ski program is another story. I was not put there by luck like my rock-guide course, but I earned it by skiing almost every day for two seasons. Maybe I did not have the same résumé as the other candidate, but I'd had my share of backcountry tours. Unfortunately, I had my stroke the autumn before.

When I turn my mind on something, I invest 100 percent of my energy in it. Instead of focusing on a bunch of things at the same time, I was all about the Cubs, cross-country skiing, my expedition, my climbing and my skiing in a different stage of my past life. More recently, my books, my movies and website. Basically, anything to get recognized.

I was locked down for what I really am. People who don't know my background kept me held up, saying I have a mental disorder. I sure know I'm not sick. Maybe hospitals need to do a better screening before locking down people.

Especially if the person is insisting that he doesn't belong there and refusing to take pills. I felt pretty normal, but everybody was trying to figure me out. One positive thing was the free food. For the rest, it was a total waste of time.

Letter to the MEDIA:

This is my last attempt! I wrote a big letter about the discrimination I face. I will say it; you're part of the problem. I have a painting in an exhibition at Contemporary Calgary until March 15th.

I signed a major book deal that would make many writers jealous. The book will be out of this autumn. I invite you to read it!

By the way, I'm very disabled. Paralyzed on one hemisphere right!

My book is essential to me. Producing my movie is also very important. My ex-wife doesn't believe it is so important, so we don't see and communicate with each other.

I landed a major book deal. Olympia is based in London and will distribute my book worldwide. I'm the only one who believed in it. If it were up to others, the book would be dead a long time ago. I will produce my movie. It's too good to leave the idea to stay just in my imagination. That new boost of confidence is because I'm successful with my book after a decade of rejection.

I thought that I was in another crisis when I wrote my book. I was sure not, just highly motivated. I know that because I'm in crisis right now, and my level of confidence is beyond anything I experienced in 1998-2000.

The last time, I was so motivated that I did not fear anything. I was briefly like the Bruce Lee of mountaineering. Then my ex-wife came into my life. I chose love and forgot about expeditions. All my mountaineering heroes picked the mountain first, love second. Of course, they say they will never die, and they will always be there for their loved one, but is it really the case?

Before I met her, I was fearless. It's a good thing she came in my life because I would be dead. I don't regret anything, and if it were to do it again, I would redo it without any hesitation. I was happy, and I did not care any more about expeditions (my dream at one point). I really loved her. I believe mountaineering is full of selfish individuals. After winter on Denali, I became a regular dude who likes to spice it up once in a while. I was fearful!

I'm maybe different but not crazy at all. My book is an incredible test piece of what my life represents. No bullshit, no flowers to mask the reality. Read part of *Epilogue* to find out about my stay in the psychiatric unit (select "epilogue" from the menu @ nevergiveup.online)

My movie is one of a kind. The idea came to me with the ski movie *Attack of la Nina*. Search it on YouTube (it is available in integral). The concept is straightforward, twenty-eight songs, twenty-eight life events (select movie for a demo on the menu @ nevergiveup.online). Music is unbelievable, super good with the remix of *Linkin Park*. The film will be in the place I recollected my journeys. Sorry, but the film will need to travel to Weir Qc, Aconcagua, Ecuador, Mckinley… One track of sound for the French and English. The movie is like it happened. When I speak French, there will be subtitles for the English version and vice versa. The film is mostly shot with a GoPro. Any climber can take the lead; there doesn't need to be competent actors but competent climbers. The movie is from my perspective, so you will not see my face but what I see from my own eyes. It is a unique concept, and that is what will make the movie so good.

I'm super creative, and people take me for *cou-cou* for it. I like to think they are insane for thinking I'm crazy. All the people that I care about, they don't talk to me anymore. I believe there is a significant glitch in the society— more with the medical world, justice, media and film industry.

I asked my doctor to fix the big mess I'm in, but he can't. He referred me to a social worker. They are the ones who supposed to get me out of this situation. My appointment with the worker lasted not even five minutes. She can't help me with my issues. Basically, I need to deal with all this myself. It's a good thing, I can write on the computer because I would lose the battle, otherwise.

There is no justice for someone who can't communicate clearly. I contacted about twenty-five lawyers. Small to big, Calgary to Edmonton, they all ignored me. Most did not bother to answer me.

The media are protecting Alberta Health Services, so basically, they are boycotting me. I contacted them three times but I received no answer.

Two years ago, I applied to the Filmmaker Workshop at the Banff Center. I registered with a specific project, which probably makes me the only one prepared like that. I had all the requirements with my ten (professionally made by Shaw) episodes that I produced. I believe that twenty got in and there were five that were rejected. I was one of the five. I did

(YouTube) *My Extreme Summer* from my desk.

This year, I applied to the VIMFF Adventure Film Grant for producing the movie of my dreams. I got two confirmations and then, nothing. It turned out that they threw my application in the garbage. If they had read it, they would see it is crazy good. The story is about bullying, and it is made for all schools in Canada and the US.

I've been applying for years at different festivals. My closest chance has been (YouTube) Adapt screener. I found out this year, they were taking my money, and most of them didn't judge me. I figured this one out with (YouTube) *Remy's Life*.

Being so lonely, I adopted a rescue kitten with three legs. Like me, he has significant challenges to face. Lucky him, he found somebody who will love him for what he is, a cat. I'm only expecting for what I am, a human being and not a disabled person.

I would like it if you don't broadcast my news with my ex-wife. In case she wants to sue my sorry ass. She might get more luck with a lawyer since she can communicate easily.

The Idea

First, I was so pissed off at the media to turn its back on me. Because, of course, after the letter, I heard nothing. Then, I started to joke with my friends that they must think that I will start a revolution like the Hunger Games. At least if they didn't think it was funny, I laugh out loud at the idea. It is so absurd and ridiculous, that is pure science fiction. March 5th, 2020, was the day. I slept on the idea. I woke up on my birthday, more thinking that was not so ridiculous after all. Thank you to the media for rejecting me; you are the only one to blame if there is somebody to blame. For sure, I won't speak to the media. If they think they will clear their hands, I say not that easy. My redemption has begun, I refuse to communicate with them, but if they want to talk about me, well... good on me! I will go to talk shows, but I'm determined to get the news to pay for protecting Alberta Health Services and not reporting the big picture. I thought they would be all over my case of discrimination, but instead, they hide me very well. I tried four times to get their attention, and not even one responded 😠!

Here is How it Will Work!

After sleeping with the idea, I realize how much people could be saved in this world with my diet. Millions and millions in Third World countries could have a fair chance. We are in 2020, and while the technologies get so far advanced, there is a significant portion of this world starving to death. This is what I mean by being smart! Actually, I'm not thinking of a new idea, I just see the world from another perspective, and I'm not scared to bring it up. Pure North was providing the homeless and me with super-strong vitamins. Somebody researched what we need. I just take the idea and expose it to the whole world. I found out that my immune system is super strong by pure luck by having a bad lung infection. If I would never be sick, I would never know.

A revolution is on our doorstep. A peaceful, quiet one with no protests and quite different to what we could imagine, that will be achieved by everyone, getting some vitamins, eating less and enjoying still a real meal a day. The weight of the population will go down, and heart disease will go down. The hospitals will get less crowded. Eventually, they will need to lay off people. Countries will be more prosperous, and the tax will be lowered. Insurance will be cheaper because of the enormous bill they will save in useless pills. With all that extra business to vitamin companies, the price will go down. If not, if they are trying to make more money and they should be shamed and boycotted.

Instead, they should be a conscious part of the human community and donate vitamins for the Third World and homeless people. If we all work together, we can really change for the best.

All of this can only happen over time. Let's take vitamins first and let the rest figure it out over time. If you were planning to start a career in health, maybe you will need to reconsider it. There will always be hospitals for trauma; they will be just smaller. Perhaps we will see some professions going dead. I have some really close friends who are dietitians, I'd hate to see them unemployed, but there are so many lives that could be saved that even they should take the inconvenience positively.

Food banks and human society like World Vision and Unicef could help way more by buying vitamins and distributing super drinks (Ensure, Boost or generic equivalents) than distributing low-quality food. Sure, it fills a hole but as nutriment... it is total crap! They could give dog food, and it won't make a difference. I know, I used to hang out at the Mustard Seed, an organization helping homeless people.

The reality, I'm a dreamer. Thinking all this could be possible; it gives me a sense of being a member of the big community of humanity. Maybe I won't be able to convert the whole world, but I am sure that a lot will jump on the bandwagon. I'm sure sales of the vitamin will go up; hopefully, companies will provide vitamins for the Third World for free. The frenzy of the coronavirus is in full swing. People are scared, but not me! I don't know for sure, but I think the virus doesn't stand a chance against my white cells.

Sure, you can spend a fortune on vitamins, but I buy the cheapest one. I watch for sales and, that way, I make sure to boost my health for the minimum amount. The only one where I don't watch the price is my extreme probiotic. Let's say I could buy a lot a vitamin for the price of one month of probiotics.

Ten Months off the Methylphenidate; Life is Good!

Ten months off the methylphenidate and I still suffer from taking the drug, but it is improving every day. I bet one and a half years, and I will always be recovering from the medication, but I will be really close to brake off jail. My eyesight has improved significantly. There is a clock on the joystick of my electric wheelchair, but I never looked at it because I could not see the numbers. It was the same for the odometer. Now, not even when I'm trying hard, I see clearly the numbers. I could see even smaller numbers with ease. My eye still jumps but way, way better than it used too. At hockey, for example, there is a minimal difference in the first period, about 50% better on the second and 100% better in the third. In fact, I see the full period and after the game until bedtime.

I guess I'm doomed to take potent probiotics forever. I was hoping, after two months, I will resume the twelve billion cells. That was just an illusion because, after four months, I still need crazy sixty billion cells. I guess that is something new, never heard about because it is not listed anywhere of possible side effects. I manage quite well with my probiotics. My bank account is the only one that suffers. When I have heartburn, instead of taking useless pills, I take extra probiotics, and it does the trick. When I eat out, I take thirty billion cells and twenty milligrams of Famotidine. That way, I can eat whatever I want and not worry about my digestive problem.

My foot is finally normal after ten months. I used, for the last time, Drysol, this past week. Drysol is basically, aluminum chloride. The same stuff that was in antiperspirants and was banned years ago because it can lead to losing your mind. I used Extra Strength for one year and a half, then five months of Regular Strength and finally, Mild Strength for one month. My foot problem is a thing of the past. I can't go totally reckless with it but anyway, good enough too finally, after three years, be free of the restraint.

My sweating at night is a thing of the past. I don't need to shower every night before bed. Last time, I check in with you about the subject, it was fine to skip a shower, but it was less than ideal. I could still sleep all right, but I had the feeling of being kind of gross the following day. Now, after ten months of recovery, I actually sleep better after I skip a shower, and I don't feel gross at all. I could even skip two showers; I sleep all right, but I feel like, when I skipped a shower before, kind of gross. That means I can go sleep out the Friday and Saturday. I did not want to go sleeping out two nights in a row without a shower. Because, by the second day, my foot would freeze without washing, but now my foot is back to normal.

Conclusion

Because of the coronavirus outbreak, I'm in a rush to get that book to publication. I know, it is on the short side and maybe drier than *Never Give Up!* I consider that manuscript more important than his predecessor. For all the reasons being, I include this book with my first (under the same cover). Sell it as a package deal, I say. I always think outside the box. I wanted to do something special for my first book. Now, I will do something special, all right; I bet I'm the only one ever who wrote those kinds of books to have two books with one launch. People took me for crazy; from the beginning, I've been honest. I never imagined I would have so much trouble because I did not think something was wrong with me. Hopefully, people like Dr Nuts will listen more to their patients instead of putting us all in the same boat. I swear, you complicated my life extremely because my struggles grew exponentially after my hospital stay.

I'm trying to get my doctor to read my text about my diet: think outside the box. I called him and texted him three times. I want him to read this document because I believe sincerely that I might hold the key to the coronavirus. I did my part, and now, the ball isn't in my camp. He answered me to relax my brain. Here is another example that people don't take me seriously. This is also ironic, the same guy that the system shit so much on him, might actually save the world. I deposit that manuscript to Olympia before I test against the coronavirus. Because, if it is working, I suspect it will be out of control, and if not… at least I will still have a book. Hopefully, my doctor will find five minutes to read my essay. If you never heard of me, it is because of one of those two things; it doesn't work, or my article went unnoticed.

This book is much more dryer than my first book. My ghostwriter needed to go her way for a personal reason. I wish her good luck, and I want to say thank you for sticking with me for so long. Now, I feel more confident in my writing and decided to leave out, still 50% of my ghostwriter work. Anyway, I feel my writing is good enough, and editors from Olympia will handle my text anyway. I really can't explain how I can write in a second language. If you meet me, you will find out that I can't hide that I'm from Quebec "*la belle province*."

Epilogue II

I've been isolating, now, for 3 ½ months. Life is so dull! My attitude to go get her is replaced by laziness. I have absolutely nothing to do. Good thing I've got my book deal because I don't think I would survive without a significant breakdown. Now, I will have my book, and I'm playing a bunch of scenarios in my head. Bring it on, I could be isolating a while longer, and I will always have my right mind.

What I'm doing? Not much except killing time doing art. Thanks to Indefinite Arts for their Zoom sessions over the internet. I could assist to 4 x 40 minutes Monday to Friday. They rescue me after the first month. Without them… I cannot imagine. I go over my comfort zone by drawing. It is the only thing mess-free that I can do. I suck, but I don't care! I made the cover of I smell a peaceful revolution. I did two practices run before I was ready for the real thing. Some people might do a piece like it very quickly and not overthinking. I needed to be extra focused and with precision. The drawing does not seem to be calculated, but for sure, it took me a lot of time and control.

I play an ongoing game that lasts close to one year. I played TRAVIAN a couple of years ago, and I drifted from the challenge because it was too much time-consuming. I have the war zone open all the time on my computer. It is a very, very serious past time. I thought that I knew a lot about Travian's world. Well, this round, I realized that I'm still very green! I was successful in my previous round only by luck and perhaps my dictation. I was with the strongest alliance, and people were too scared to attack. This time, I'm with a weaker union, and now, I'm bait for the other player.

I need to take a nap every afternoon if I want to make it to ten o'clock. One hour would be enough, but I usually go for two. I'm so bored that the time goes faster sleeping. After the crisis, I don't know if I would have the energy to get off my ass. I did not anticipate that one day, I will say that I'm lazy.

I watch movies every evening. I'm only able to watch comedies like American Pie, Zoolander, Seth Rogan's films, etc... Other, more serious stories put me to sleep. Some people may think it is so stupid; I say that it is pure entertainment.

Now, the post Methylphenidate period. Bad news for the one that thought that my gastric acid problem would be gone with time. I'm forced to take sixty billion probiotics, perhaps, for the rest of my life.

My foot his way better than it was. Unfortunately, what seemed promising, got a little worse over time but nothing to compare before. I don't need Drysol any more. It is normal to some degree, but when it freezes, I don't worry about it and suck it up. I already know that my pain is kind of a phantom, and I don't freak out because my foot is cold. This is doing the job inside my four walls. With some precaution, I will be just fine going out.

My eye is way better, and there is not even a comparison with before. I'm taking CBD oil for it. For a while, it was cure at 99%, but I got used to the dose, and I need more, but it is too expensive for now.

I still take a shower before bed, especially with the warmer temperature of the season. I sleep with pyjamas pants, a thick sweatshirt and my window open. Like before, I like cold temperatures, but not like before, I like the warmth of my covers over my head. I never sweat, even if I wear very warm PJ. I was so tough to the cold and now so sensitive. Something was wrong with me.

I was so pissed off first at the stupid COVID-19. I sure have a lack of respect for the virus. I think the world is going insane. I'm not scared at all by it; I wish I could have the illness to prove my diet to everyone. My Doctor never followed through, my brother is to scare to say anything, and my Naturopath is simply speechless. Frustrated, I made a post on Facebook but had only very hostile insults. Then, Indefinite Arts sessions came to my rescue. I realized a little bit after the Paralympic are push in 2021. I will be able to do my traverse because this book will be out. Without the book, it is impossible to make people believe. I made a beautiful website; I'm good with that kind of stuff (www.driveforparalympic.com).

I can't wait to get more ink. With time, my design evolves and includes both arms. The climbing helmet, carabiner will remain on my left complete by a sketch of a wheelchair and the planet. A sit-ski, Alter-G, audiobook and mountains will go on my right. I have space vacant for, eventually, scuba tank, mask and fin. The last three will wait if I produce my TV show on scuba diving (tandem) in the most beautiful places around the world. I have another TV show that I wish to create. Me going to do all those unusual activities like water sliding, go-kart, laser fighting, etc... I guess I was really productive on my smart pill.

I did not have my cleaner for the entire crisis. I thought that I was retired for life of home duties. I was able to do my laundry. It did not matter if it took me a long time, something to do. I realized then how little garbage I was producing. I went 44 days with the same bag in my twenty-eight-liter bin. I know exactly how long it was because I had a massive pile of empty Meal on Wheels plastic dishes for recycling. I realized then that I was on something big and not super weird, like my theory with health. I think I will have more success with my environmentally friendly idea. It took me two days to build a website for it (www.habits4planet.com).

I'm not alone in my isolation. My best buddy Cam is with me. It is pure luck that I have such a loyal friend with me. Cam got older (almost one year). He sleeps, every night on the window sill, by my bed. He was simply too young to jump, and I did not know any better. He still likes to play with is food but eat a couple of times a day and not during the night.

I think I won't have any financial problems any more. I will buy everything I need like a van and I will get a house in Canmore. I will donate the rest to causes involving the disabled! I don't believe in piling up money at the bank. My dream building would be a nature house! Not familiar at all in North America but more popular in Europe. It will be a building inside a giant dome, a greenhouse. I am eliminating the need for a bunch of expensive elements and a central heating system. My house will have an apartment in the basement for my private caregiver/gardener/driver. All the nature houses on the net are equipped with a wood fireplace. Mine won't release any gas in the atmosphere. It will be warm with portable oil radiator heater, anyway, that type of building is inexpensive heating because of the greenhouse effect. I would need central air conditioning to regulate my temperature. I had trouble with the warm night for more than ten years, and I will fix the issue forever. Because of the high consumption of energy, the ideal set up would be solar panels. My ultimate dream would be off the grid and with no gas release in the atmosphere. This type of home is the only way to make sure my foot won't freeze, and once I moved in, I really don't care about the pandemic or not. I see my old days spending a lot of time at home. I will move somewhere where I can enjoy nature from home.

I had precisely the same vision three years ago, and I told my plan to my caregiver, but we all know how receptive she was. People may think I have impossible dreams. Well, everything seems possible now, don't you think? I'm ready to forget her, but she should have confidence in me to make a union. Somebody, I'm not prepared to forget yet is Jass. When I needed you the most, you were not there. I needed to fight my way out all alone. I need more time to digest, and I will call you when I'm ready.

Luckily, I made this book on the Methylphenidate. It's been a year I stop, and my memory has a bunch of glitches. I kind of remember what I wrote in this book, but all the details are erased from my mind. Before, I had no problem remembering the small aspect, even from my youth, like it had happened yesterday. This book is a product of a mutant. I thought that I was so smart to remember everything. It was the pill that gave me the tool to finish this masterpiece; otherwise, I would not be able to write my memories. And Doctor Smart wanted to put me back on the pill after my hospital stay. Good for me that I told him:" No way!"

07/19/20

It is all making sense! It turned out; I'm normal like million other individuals but unique in a way. When I was a kid, I have always been top of my class in math at elementary. At high school, the trouble started. One year, I had my focus somewhere else than math. I failed with the worse mark of my class for the first semester. In the second semester, I got buddy with the teacher because he was a massive fan of music from the 70s. I finished the semester with the best grade of my class with a 99%. At college, I couldn't wrap my head around the final math class, my only course missing from graduating. Story short, I'm ADD (Attention Deficit

Disorder). I got never diagnose because I was burning off my extra energy by training for cross country skiing.

I started to put the piece of this very complicated puzzle Friday after my, not so much important drawing. I cannot explain how it turned out so good. Remember, drawing is not my cup of tea. Then, I realized that I must be a genius (not seriously but more seriously later).

I started to google search "ADD and genius," and my attention landed on "There's Genius in ADD." I realized then that most patients are on Ritalin or Methylphenidate. The study doesn't state the following, but it is what it is going on. The ADD without the chemical=can still functions normally (somewhat). ADD + pill=genius in some case. I bet millions of people are smarter, but only a small percentage of genius, low enough to be unnoticed. I say our world is filled with people use to take or is taking a smart pill. It would be interesting to see how much people took the medication on the art scene (music, painting, writer, movie making, etc.).

Regarding my situation, because I took such a big dose of smart, and this for twelve years, my mind became unexpectedly developed. When I switch my brain to art, movie making, book, website, music, Kung Fu and more, I become so focus on the task that I don't see the time fly by. I always seek to be the best. Slowly, I transformed in to be what I am, a genius. I wrote this book, not knowing about my ADD disorder.

It is time to unleash my rant. I will always be at a colossal disadvantage when I'm drawing or painting. Not so much in my mixed media only because I'm the only one or if they're more, I never heard about them. I wish people would recognize that disability art is not only for recreation. I seek to be recognized in another category of art. It is about time someone exposes the truth. There are two art categories, one for able body and one for disabled. I'm sick and tire of being judge with able bodies. I believe I do incredible art, but compare to an able buddy, I sucked! I don't care if I'm doing good art or not. I'm stuck at home with the only possibility of drawing. I consider watercolour pencils to be familiar to drawing. I attribute to arts that I survive this difficult period. I will resume my mixed media when I go back to the studio at Indefinite Arts. I don't think about making art to be famous when I'm making it, but it sure would be nice. I feel it doesn't matter how hard or good you could be, when you are disabled, people don't take you seriously and this, in about anything.

07/20/20

The previous is not only what happened to me. I did not spend seven or eight years writing this book by failing to tell you what I became. The facts are all the same, except I did not tell you how smart I am. Well, this must sound pretentious, but believe me when I say I'm not. I'm super, super bright! I say that is beyond just be a genius; I'm a mutant, and that is what I am. I can access only my smartest when I'm in the zone. Otherwise, I'm still at a disadvantage to an able body, but at least, I reduced the massive gap between us. I have no issue at all when there are people around, and I don't consider to be more intelligent. Quite often, I think people are more genius than I am but when I'm in the zone… Watch out! I'm quite something. If I need to be in the zone and there are people around, I must act like the biggest asshole. I have no emotion in my face and my voice. Just ask the nurses who helped me during my shower during my hospital stay. Sorry, been so cold was not my intention.

When I went to the hospital, it came to my mind to lie, but I really wanted to sleep, so I didn't. Probably my dumbest move ever. I wasn't lying Dr Nuts and Jass; I'm not kidding, I'm the smartest guy on the planet. All this could be avoided because I told Dr. Nuts precisely what is wrong with me, but of course, he absolutely did not care and ignored it. He was using his power to make my life difficult and tag me as manic. I got the weirdest side effects with Methylphenidate, even though I'm scared to use any drugs, It is probably still a proper medication, but Doctors need to do a better screening. It seems like they give the pill as it was candy. All this happened because I was stuck with a wheelchair with the sensibility on. My problem is not new; I'm in the zone or else, I crash. I've been like this for thirteen years. I "walked" my life strait for forty-one years. I deserve my redemption because of all the "abuse" I endure. I kept quiet and always got better. With my book, it is the first time I'm wining, and it feels so good that people will accord me the attention I deserve.

I realize I will always have to fight for my rights; I just hope I did not do this book for anything, that it will actually help me going forward in life. I'm a human being, a weird one, but still a person.

Appendix

Helpers with my struggle over the years (as per year 2020)

Hospital:

Calgary Brain Injury Program —
Foothills Medical Center
1403 29 Street NW
Calgary, Alberta
T2N 2T9

The Centennial Center for Mental Health and Brain Injury Rehabilitation center: mentalhealthexcellence.ca
South Calgary Health Center
31 Sunpark Plaza SE
Calgary, Alberta
T2X 3W5

Discussion group:

Southern Alberta Brain Injury Society:	SABIS sabis.ab.ca
Stroke Recovery Association of Calgary — Young Survivors	sracalgary.com/young_survivors

Sport/recreation:

YMCA Calgary:	www.ymcacalgary.org
camp horizon:	easterseals.ab.ca/CampSite/EasterSealsCampHorizon.aspx info@easterseals.ab.ca

Outdoor activities:

Rocky Mountain Adaptive	rockymountainadaptive.com info@rockymountainadaptive.com

Sports:

Kung Fu: Canadian Wing Chun Kung Fu Association	wingchun-canada.com
Alpine skiing: CADS	cadscalgary.ca
Power hockey: CPHL	powerhockey.ca info@powerhockey.ca
ACPSA (power soccer and boccia)	acpsa.ca contact@acpsa.ca
Disabled Sailing Association of Alberta	dsaalberta.org info@dsaalberta.org
Wheelchair rugby: Inferno	www.calgaryinferno.com guiry.inferno@hotmail.com
Sledge hockey: Calgary Sledge Hockey Association	www.calgarysledgehockey.ca info@calgarysledgehockey.ca

Others:

Alter-G (anti-gravity treadmill): Foot jax	footjax.com
Art program: In-Definite Arts	indefinitearts.com ida@indefinitearts.com
Calgary Co-op Home Health	calgarycoop.com/home_health
Dentist: Dr Harbison	harbisondental.com
Physiotherapy: Tower Physio	towerphysio.ca
Shaw TV Calgary Channel 10 Community Access Programming	shaw.ca/shawtv/calgary/
Meals on Wheels	mealsonwheels.com
Accessable Housing Calgary	accessiblehousing.ca
Calgary Legal Guidance	clg.ab.ca
Calgary Animal Rescue Society	**trish@calgaryanimalrescue.com**
CUPS	info@cupscalgary.com
Apartment: Vivenda 56	vivenda56.com

Manufactured by Amazon.ca
Bolton, ON